AMERICAN PEOPLE
and
DEMOCRACY

by
ANONYMOUS

USDF PUBLISHING

USDF Publishing

ISBN: 978-0-578-23433-5

PRINTED IN THE UNITED STATES OF AMERICA

"This essay is dedicated to Americans of all races, cultures and ages, who push, haul, teach, learn, drive, drill, heal, serve, preach, demolish, build, create, write, compose, and invent - every American. This book would not exist without you."

Anonymous
(Authors of American People and Democracy)

AMERICAN PEOPLE AND DEMOCRACY

"If liberty means anything at all, it means the right to tell people what they do not want to hear."

"We have now sunk to a depth at which the restatement of the obvious is the first duty of intelligent men."

George Orwell

TABLE OF CONTENTS

PROLOGUE

"In 2020, the Democrat party won the election. We wish President-Elect Joe Biden and Vice President Elect Kamala Harris a warm welcome as we did the previous administrations, all of whom, in one way or another, made good, as well as bad decisions. We continue to agree and disagree on which were fruitful and which were not.

The 2020 election result is problematic for a lot of American people. One of the more tragic and perplexing issues that our leadership is facing is dealing with Covid-19 and its impact on most of our assumed socio-economic structures.

The new team in the White House will need the support of everybody to contain and eliminate this monster. It will be difficult. We are, it seems more than ever, drowning in partisanship, intolerance, and dogmatism to the point of social violence erupting. Things have deteriorated to the point that it feels as if Democracy itself is at stake.

This essay attempts to seek out the reasons for this, and to shed light on some alarming problems that have been in the making for the last thirty to forty years, rendering the election of Donald Trump not a fluke, as some would see it as, or a historical accident, but its result.

The 2020 election result was full of oddities.
Many of the people who were responsible for Donald Trump's election in 2016 are the same ones who aided his defeat in 2020. The oddity is that the political platform of the Democrats did not change. It is the same one popularized four years ago; it's just that now, it is marketed it in a more radical, polarized, and aggressive fashion.

Democrats heartily won the popular vote but lost eight seats in the house which seems contradictory. Does it mean, as Ann Coulter, a conservative media commentator, said, "Americans want Trumpism without Trump?"

Does it mean that Joe Biden was elected mainly as a result of Covid-19, which put millions of people out of work? Our contradictions are deep; every day we witness the tearing up of our American values to the point that there is no more "Social Contract" between us - no civic bind.

This has led to the uncertainty of what we are as a people, and has opened the door to an imperial presidency underpinned by limited massive economic interests that don't seem to value democracy.

This essay, "The American People and Democracy" sets out to clarify the situation we find ourselves in, in part, by reviewing the impact that the last 4 critical years have had on our democracy.

We published our book under Anonymous. Still we can give some information about who they are:

American citizen from the center left, Democrat voters, Progressist-Humanist who thru business contacts, casual encounters, meetings, traveling, seminars, dinners, even dating etc. realized that they were sharing the same preoccupation about the future of our Country. What was the most noticeable for them was the extreme diversity of socio-politico-economic backgrounds between all of them and still sharing the same anguish and worries about the future. Several dozens of those people kept in contact and started to collect and exchange information useful for an in-depth article for a good magazine. But due to the increase of information it mutated into a memo of around 70 pages. Getting even more documents/information show us that all the issues we were concern by were deeply linked. Our book, an Essay, is the introduction for five books titled Bad-feminism and Democracy, Sexualists and Democracy, Radical-Minorities and Democracy, Infosphere/media and Democracy and Mega-Corps and Democracy. None one of them is interested by any kind of media circus, which will, invariably, take away the meaning of any arguments from the book.

All those people, who want to remain anonymous, contributed one way or the other, to the book. We understand their desire, since 65% of American citizen are afraid to share their political view as it makes them and their family vulnerable to all type of aggressions by the vicious, intolerant, bigoted, dogmatic, racist we exposed in our book.

We asked a friend of a friend to publish it.

The book's title is:

American People and Democracy, which is the first of a series of books on the current political environment in the United States of America.

This book serves as an introduction to the ideas which will be the subjects of the next books in the series. In the following books, we will be exploring "Radical Feminism and Democracy," "Sexualists and Democracy," "Radical Minorities and Democracy," "Infosphere/Media and Democracy," and "Conglomerates and Democracy."

This book is separated into several sections; brief descriptions below:

LEXICON: Reference of key words and phrases, as they are used in the book.

INTRODUCTION: Statement of purpose and goal of this book

FOUNDATIONS: Brief summary of some of the historical sources of the ideas, philosophy, doctrines and ideologies upon which the ideas in this book are founded

RADICAL FEMINISM: (also referred to as "Badfem" in the book).
An abbreviated exploration of the deviance and

corruption of the social movement known as "Feminism" and the devastating consequences that corruption has wreaked upon American society.

SEXUALISTS: The group or groups of people who utilize political power to empower the societal rejection and ostracization they have experienced in the past because of their identification as people with alternate sexualities, differing from what we term "normative," which is to say, the majority who 'identify as heterosexual," aka: heterosexual.

MINORITIES OF MINORITIES: The self-appointed "authorities" who claim defining mastery of their own particular group. They are at the extremes, manifest in small clans of social militants who are prone to extreme posturing and use the all-ready media to amplify their messages of hatred of mainstream culture.

INFOSOPHERE/MEDIA: A quick overview of the evolution of the media business into the "Infosphere." This media infosphere has had a huge impact on the evolution/devolution of America. The constant influx of factual news co-mingled with fake/alt-news and propaganda disguised as advertising, have rendered it impossible to conduct coherent, informed dialogue among people and social groups, the consequences of which are divisiveness, dogmatism, and intolerance, precluding any hope of building a common future.

SUPERCONGLOMERATES: A discussion of the evolution of neo-economic liberalism which is now a direct threat to democracy. American society has up until now, rested on Judicial, Executive and Legislative branches. This is an exploration of the ways in which Super-Conglomerates undermine and corrupt the strength of these deep, foundational American driving forces.

Conclusion: Badfeminism, sexualism and radical racist minorities aren't part of the progressive left. These groups are small, from the fringes of our society, and have been given and are being given a disproportionately large presence in our culture through the mainstream media. They try the replace our values with their claims. Neo-liberalism, which doesn't need any, is giving all help necessary. The consequences of extreme laissez faire of the market economy resulted in the concurrent emergence of conglomeration and globalization.

We are exploring whether the left-leaning political apparatus is qualified to reintroduce some decency, basic logic and coherence in our society. Does that 'Left' have the will to put back strong anti-trust legislation into our economic life? Are they willing to take on the consortium of conglomerates which control the infosphere/media complex?

We all must wake up to the fact that they aren't our friends, that the uber-conglomerates aren't in favor of democracy at all. In fact, they live within our country and lie in wait within our socio-political system to poison our democratic ways of thinking, our democratic values and, once this is accomplished, will take over our country. This scenario has played out many times before in history – and, very simply, leads to fascism. This is what our book is all about.

LEXICON

"To live is to think." Cicero

WARNING to all people who think that their feelings are more important than their thinking, please don't read this book! There is no safe space for you in it.

Our book is about bad feminism, sexualism, radical racist minorities, dysfunctional media and overwhelming economic power of conglomerates. The consequences of their politic in our society are catastrophic.

Even if it is not an academic book, you can detect in it references from academia to support our arguments. Most of them are illustrated with examples taken from the daily lives of American people.

List of buzzwords:
A buzzword is a word or phrase, often an item of jargon, that is fashionable at a time or in a specific context. They are used by lazy people who, instead of explaining their ideas, rely on a catch phrase that is supposedly pregnant

with significance, but it's just their way of skimming the surface with their arguments and avoiding an examination of an issue in-depth.

-LIBERALISM?

Are we liberal? "We traditionally called ourselves "Progressive-Liberals". But, recently, some of us have found the term, "liberal" to be debased and discredited, so they have started to drop that descriptive, and use only the term, "Progressive". Neo-Liberal, neo-liberal economist is what we are not." (USDF)

- Misogynists hate women, we are phylogenies who like them.
- Misandrists hate men, we are philandrists who like them.

- Sexists: If you aren't a radical feminist, as a woman you are just a stupid cow who doesn't understand, since the beginning of time, your condition as slaves. If a man, you can't be anything else than sexist, misogynist pigs etc. mainly because you will never be able to satisfy the numerous and contradictory needs of some modern women who expect to "get it all" from men who "just don't get it."

- Misogyny and sexism are now synonyms. It's a strong and vicious combination of two buzz words, synonyms of hatred, enmity and disgust of the other sex. It is used often by radical feminists.

- Victimhood:
Calling yourself a victim at this moment has nothing to

do with having been raped, murdered, robbed, or other real-life catastrophic events. No, it is a new concept relating to one's feelings. One feels oneself a victim of some perceived aggression, some bigoted or sexist behavior. It is a feeling of unhappiness, of discomfort with yourself and your life. One has strong feelings that somebody, not you of course, is responsible for your feelings and your misfortune.

- Paternalism:
Paternalism as opposed to patriarchy reflects an unresolved feminist oedipal complex.
"If I've killed one man, I have killed two
The vampire who said he was you
And drank my blood for a year,
Seven years, if you want to know.
Daddy, you can lie back now."
Sylvia Plath, Daddy

- Patriarchy:
Patriarchy started to dissolve around 1850. The impact of the Industrial Revolution emptied the house of men who went to work in factories. Still, the word patriarchy is used invariably in feminist literature and proclamations for political advantage. Patriarchy is, for them, a very useful villain.

- Racism:
After having a president from a minority elected twice, people expected a tone-down of the racial rhetoric. It has the opposite effect and we saw an explosion of racist organizations carrying racist ideologies like whiteness, etc.

-Homophobia: distaste of homosexual people. Phobia means fear of OR aversion of. "All homosexuals are sinners and will burn in Hell." Anonymous signs on a street manifestation.

-Heterophobia: distaste of heterosexual people. Phobia means fear of OR aversion of. "All heterosexual sex is rape." Quote from Andrea Dworkin.

-Gender Racism is a combination of gender discrimination and racism, from the radical feminist, sexualist, and radical minorities as a new socio-racist concept. It is the fusion of gender as a cultural concept and Whiteness as a racial theory.

Our own classification of who is what since feminism is a vast subject with many subsets.
List of our archenemy:
- Talibfem who are as intolerant, vicious, fanatic, as their Taliban friends from Afghanistan, who are the male version of them.
- Ratfem, are between the talibfem fem and the Radfem.
- Radfem, radical feminists which after three waves of feminism must face the fact that their ideology is drowning.
- We will write mainly about the three above and regroup them under bad-fem.

List of our frenemy:
- So-SoFem exists as well, since we live in a democracy. They certainly have the right to express

their opinions. We welcome and share some of the latest since we are part of the feminist movement.

List of our Goodfem:
- All individuals or groups of people, who understand that our book is a feminist book.
- Veganfem, yogafem, dietfem, acroyogafem, Coucoufem, freakyfem, psychofem etc. aren't a concern of ours.

Sexualists, LGBTQ+++ etc.
The only specificity of the latest is that they relate sexually to their own gender. Many seminal psychologists have written on the matter such as Freud, Jung, and Betty Joseph to name a few. Please note that we are not the least bit interested in the sexuality of individuals, but by the politic followed by their leadership. Regarding LGBTQ+++ denomination, we think that the G of 'GAY' is now totally obsolete, it will be replaced by H for Homo since lesbians don't call themselves 'Happies', bisexual 'Flipflops', Transgender 'Sliders' etc. LHBTQ+++ is, in 2020, much more appropriate.

Political correctness: P.C.
A tendency by some to impose a system of acceptable and unacceptable speech/behavior. If the censorship becomes societal, the P.C. rules will become cultural. To express ourselves a certain way will control our thinking.

The use of insults:
Bad-fem, sexualists, RRM give to themselves the right to call anybody they disagree with any offensive libels they

want, "mother-f...r white ass h...!", "sexist pig", "misogynistic ass h...", "fleeting cunt" etc. Well, if it is called for, we won't hesitate to call a bad-fem, a "turd"!

Infosphere/media
Prescient writers, from Theillard de Chardin's Noosphere to Alvin Toffler and his seminal book. Luciano Floridi developed and investigated with great insight the idea of the infosphere. It includes everything related to ways of communication by sound, visual, writing. However, we are more interested in why such a magnificent tool has such a devastating effect on the way we are informed and who are responsible for it.

GAFA EU = Google, Apple, Facebook, Amazon (a convenient terminology used frequently in Europe.)

FANG US= Facebook, Amazon, Netflix, Google, the new FAANG include Apple now but keep Netflix which is not the right place for that corporation.

Confederation of Fools, aka 'the useful idiots', are all people who believe and are active in propagating any ideas from Bad feminists, sexualists, radical racist mini-minorities. Sometimes we regroup all of them under "RRM endeavor" or "RRM system" because all have the same goals.

SuperCapitalism = SuperConglos = MegaCorps:
Are the results of a conglomeration of our traditional capitalism. The people in charge of these play a worldwide economic game, where America is only a pawn on their side of the chess board, and often not their most important one.

Capitalists = are the ones playing the field in America and will be absorbed by SuperConglos soon, if they don't acknowledge that danger.

Deconstructionists = Are people who have been destroying the fundamental values of our society for more than half a century and are unable to come up with any new and constructive one.

Sympathy or compassion:
these, in our opinion, are more appropriate than empathy. Nobody can really feel what others are going through when dying of thirst crossing the desert trying to reach the US. We might be horrified and infuriated by such situations. But to actually feel the thirst, the desperation, the fear that these persons may feel? We doubt it. Of course, we support any political action which might put an end to such atrocities. We will prefer to use the words sympathy and compassion.

We didn't include any quote, pictures, videos, links from the most sick, vicious, people who call for the extermination of some of us.

INTRODUCTION

"This nation will remain the land of the free so long as it is the home of the brave." Elmer Davis

"Remember, remember always, that all of us, and you and I especially, are descended from immigrants and revolutionists." Franklin D. Roosevelt

"America will never be destroyed from the outside. If we falter and lose our freedom, it will be because we destroyed ourselves." Abraham Lincoln

"Those in power must spend a lot of time laughing at us." Alice Walker

THIS BOOK IS about a debate initiated in the 1960s by socio-political issues like the Vietnam War, the Civil Rights Movement, and the Feminist movement. The new ideas expressed in these powerful and necessary movements caused enormous stress on the social fabric of our society. We have never really recovered from that major rift; we never had a healing or a rebuilding of the unified American consensus that existed prior to these movements. During the half century that has passed, the shape and appearance of the founding ideas has drastically changed. What we are left with now, 50 years later, are the mere remnants of these groups, which have dwindled into factions, and their initially righteous ideas have now been left blowing aimlessly in the cold ashes of the original, idealistic ideologies.

During the 1968 Olympics, John Carlos and Tommie Smith, two African Americans stood on the winner's podium and accepted their medals with raised fists and bent heads, the symbol of the Black Power movement. These days, that protest has become Colin Kaepernik and Marshawn Lynch of the 2017 NFL. Peggy McKintosh, the scholar and educator who was at the forefront of inclusive education, and Andrea Dworkin, the radical feminist who first started the discussion of male privilege and power and its societal institutionalization, have now become the Rebecca Solnit's treatise about rape and male condescension to women and Linda Martin Alcoff, writing about the "future of whiteness" in today's society. Stokely Carmichael, from the 'Black Power' movement of the '70s, has morphed into Michael Eric Dyson in the 21st Century. The ideals, the politics have changed. The '60s feminist mass movement is now scattered in a multitude of vociferous, dogmatic little groups. These are all over our side of the political spectrum. They have little in common with the traditional left; they are more the ultimate expression of the decaying of the left's radical fringe.

We must seek to provide a kind of echo chamber where the frustration and exasperation of the American people can be heard loudly, and the values we hold dear, can be seen destroyed before our very eyes, because of the splintering of these initially honorable groups into self-serving factions that now are boded up by the 800-pounds gorilla called the SuperConglos, MegaCorps, SuperCapital etc.

THE STATE OF OUR LEADERSHIP

Our party leadership place blame for our situation in several places, whether it's Republicans, the Russians, Hillary Clinton's deplorables, the Chinese's, the EU etc. Some of us did forecast the results of 2016 elections, some didn't, but all of us were acutely aware of some deep trouble inside the Republican <u>and</u> Democratic Party. The latest was baffled by the election of Donald Trump. It should have put it one on one's guard about the meaning of it. They thought it was just a lucky stroke. It wasn't.

A lot of excellent books have been written about the results of that election, with detailed analysis of the context, sophisticated statistics, etc. Here, our group is trying to examine the oddities of our contemporary political life. In studying these, we gain perspective on how deep the crisis in our value system is. In the election of 2016, we witnessed a constant assault on what unifies us, and the extreme polarization of both political personalities accelerated it. After the failure of 2016, it is appalling to see the leadership of the party going about its business as usual. We don't see any shake up, clean up or shift in our politics. It's "business as usual." All people involved with the DNC in 2016 should have resigned. We need to see a strong and viable movement to replace all incompetent politicians who still remain in control of the party. We need new blood, or the party will die of anemia!

Hilary Clinton appeared satisfied that she won the popular vote by 3 million votes. This is hardly an accomplishment when she should have won the election by twenty-five million votes! She should have, with all the help received, crushed the Republican candidate the way Lyndon Johnson crushed Barry Goldwater.

Even though her campaign was intensely focused on motivating women and securing their support, 54% of women didn't vote for her, and she got only one percentage point more of the female vote than Obama, (and lost the male vote by 12 points, while Obama lost by 7). If she had lost the male vote by the same percentage as Obama, she would have been elected! Why did she do so poorly with men? There are many reasons, but one that struck us was hearing her say that, "Women have always been the primary victims of war ... women lose their husbands, their fathers, their sons in combat..." Obviously, she couldn't count on the vote of men six feet under but why didn't her campaign prevent her from speaking words so obviously divisive? Hilary had 30 years of political experience at the highest level. There is certainly more than its share of foolish feminist politics, but something is terribly wrong with a party that allows its presidential candidate to ignore and even alienate over 117 million male voters!

After our defeat, we expected the Democrat politicians to come to understand that betting only on the female electorate was a tragic mistake. The junior Senator from California, Kamala Harris, was championing a set of bills regarding incarceration only for women. There are 213,700 women incarcerated in the US., but she doesn't address the 2½ million men in prisons. If there is a "women's prisoner problem" there is an even bigger problem for men--91% bigger, in fact! Mass incarceration is an American problem, which concerns all of us, not only women! We expected something a little bit more coherent from Kamala Harris, an African American, South-Asian woman who certainly has knowledge of the devastation of the out of control incarceration on numerous minority families. (those lines were written before she was a presidential candidate, abandoned the race and was chosen as Vice-President by Joseph R. Biden.)

We face a conundrum, because we have two intelligent, well-educated women, savvy politicians, from the same political party who make the same mistake a year and half apart. What's going on? For one, it demonstrates how deep the influence of Bad-feminism theories are and how they have polluted the core of the left political culture. But even more important, when Hilary Clinton wins 589 of the wealthiest counties and Donald Trump wins 2,623, we are witnessing a drastic change in our electorate. We became the party of the rich and the Republicans have now become "the people's party" This book is an attempt to find out why and how this happened.

WHAT IS OF OUR CONCERN

We are focusing on the issues concerning only the liberal side of the political spectrum. Our current president's policies, as tempting as it might be, will not be included, because we alone are responsible for our own demise. We insist we want to focus on OUR problems, and our problems only, because the election of President Trump *is the result* of a political situation *not its cause*. We will explain why a minority of radical feminists have control over feminism, why the sexualists are running wild with political claims, why radical minorities have their community in a chokehold, why mass media and Super-Capitalism are the ones making it possible. They are critical issues we are facing now in our nation.

To make our book easy to understand we would like to be specific "we are "causalists" and our opponents are "consequentialists". We want to master, resolve our social problems, we don't want to whine and bleat about the consequences of it. We are "assimilationists," they are "separatists"; we are in favor of the "common good," they are in favor of "their specific good." (USDF)

We are more interested in ideas than feelings. Subverting reason for emotion is a dangerous mode of thought. Even if we believe that emotion and reason are of equal importance in our lives, they have distinctly different functions. Also, for us, what's more important are the fundamental reasons events have happened, not who did them. When we discuss a subject, it may focus on a book or an author that might be helpful. We will give quotes and we will mention their authors for attribution. We will choose some specific cases from our daily lives, since they illustrate quite well what the American people are going through, instead of sophisticated intellectual argument. Our group doesn't want to make this a debate about personalities. For this investigation, ideas are far more important than people. We will pinpoint, as clearly as possible, the catastrophic intellectual beliefs that put us in this situation.

We are using history as a guide when thinking about socio-economic problems. We are entirely fact-based and do not want to be overly absorbed in theoretical discussions. We are using history as a "modus operandi" to give us stronger footing to our arguments. Different "schools of history" exist, but our book isn't the place to discuss the validity of one theory over another. As Sgt. Joe Friday repeated each week on Dragnet: "Just the facts, maam, just the facts."

WHAT BEING A DEMOCRAT IS ALL ABOUT?

Being a Progressive-liberal Democrat means that we are broad-minded and tolerant. It doesn't mean that we must accept every fashionable idea from shortsighted polemicists who aren't able to understand basic political theory, or worse, unable to understand the political consequences of their actions. Those who think a sound bite is the equivalent of real thinking are more damaging to our society than the right wing they oppose. They don't accept the fact that democracy's gears are engineered with the understanding that compromise among various constituencies is foundational and is the engine behind progress. Without it we will just kill each other or live in a dictatorship. If the dogmatists were merely foolish but innocuous it would not be a problem, but unfortunately, they are organized around a dangerous rigidity espoused by intolerant militants ready to do almost anything to promote and impose their ideas.

Regrettably, we found them everywhere draped in labels like feminism, racism, sexualism and other safe havens. Let's kick them out of our party, particularly the ones who want to hire new talent for the Democratic Party "as long as they aren't straight white men"! In Idaho, let's get rid of that "Democrat" executive director who asked the DNC to train people "how to shut up their mouths if they are white." These gender racist pigs in our party must be the first ones to go; they are narrow-minded to the point of choking our political life to death.

We need here to give an example of what is of primordial importance for us. Every developed nation, other than ours, has a national system that provides affordable or free day care for children and early education, freeing women to work if they choose. We must give every child a clean and safe environment to develop through a real educational day care system. A bi-partisan, Democrat and Republican Congress elected people, must frame a *master-plan* involving health and education department people, working together to make sure that all states, all areas of our country are covered. Such a system can work only if it's based on individual responsibility *and not on irresponsibility camouflaged in a massive state organization.* We can't let some schools in difficult neighborhoods, warehouse children who get out of it without any useful education. We already have a lot of existing facilities. We want to help them work in a coherent global system of education where private and public schools can merge. Where nothing exists, we must create new facilities to reach even those in the most remote areas. In the chapter on minorities we develop that idea to the extent of making education a permanent factual reality for everybody since we must prepare ourselves to change occupations during our lifetime.

We want to make sure that nobody drops off two or three children in a house called a day care center, where the people in charge prop the children in front a TV until the parents come to get them. We need, clean, safe centers, with trained, educated people in all facilities; because it makes a huge difference, especially in the poor neighborhoods, in the way children start in life. All states must be able to remove the right to operate a day-care location where a child chokes to death on a candy because nobody knows how to do the Heimlich maneuver or CPR in that facility! We need to create a flexible system open to all people in charge of children under the guidance of a chart of obligations.

For our group, it is one example of what is wrong with U.S. policy; it is emblematic of our misguided priorities, constantly scattered around to satisfy the latest politic fad. We want to understand why the following groups, all of whom claim that they want to improve our society but are only deeply concerned by the welfare of their own. Why have we not, in 70 years, been able to establish a Nationwide Day Care System (NWDCS) which is so important for all. Naturally we have many more issues on our list like health care, employment etc., but we will focus on the first one as the absolute proof of people being involved in the common good or not. It is our litmus test.

"To summarize, our liberalism is for progressives with a spine." (USDF)

The goal of this book is to keep matters simple. We take note of what the American people are saying and will give several examples of how they perceive the state of affairs, and how they understand the consequences that the misguided policies have on their lives. We pay close attention to what people say. When we connect the dots between many different people, they all seem to result in the same observations and the same conclusions. We want to add that we are not connected in any way with the neo-liberals, who are defined by "champagne wishes and caviar dreams," as Robin Leech would say.

We would like to give the same courtesy to our children and let all future generations live peacefully in a democratic society. It's the least we can do.

ENLIGHTENMENT

PEOPLE NOT INTERESTED in history can skip this chapter.

The following is a quick overview of where the ideas or theories we argue about come from. We must do it because nothing comes from nothing. For example, liberalism is an offspring of the enlightenment, which is itself an offspring of Christianity. [See Political Theory Today, edited by David Held, Stanford University Press, 199, P.146]

From the 17th century on, the values of Judeo-Christian civilization survived many ideological and military conflicts. But a large majority of these values became secularized in the process. As Enlightenment philosophies gathered steam, they countered some teachings of organized religion, especially the most superstitious and retrograde. Seminal public-minded philosophers such as Spinoza, Voltaire, Hume, Kant, etc. all professed a kind of Deism. Even Robespierre, the epitome of a French revolutionary fanatic, tried to reintroduce a cult of a 'supreme Being'. These men didn't have a problem with God, but they did have serious disputes with the church. The Ten Commandments were fine; they provided organizing principles throughout the centuries to help people live successful lives. There is some difference in interpretation among Jews and Christians but we, more or less, all agree on our basic values and "the modern creed of democracy is to be understood as a secularized version of the most elementary tenets of Christian theology.... the conception of the common good is the secularized version of the Divine Order." [P.147]

For our group, secularism never had enough ambition to replace "religion," but it became a political solution that asked us to stop killing each other, live together in peace, and maintain our personal convictions. This was no small thing. The violence of the European religious wars was such that historians estimate the loss of lives in Germania to be around 25% of the total population. To frame this in more contemporary American terms, we are talking about a loss of 80,000,000 people!

When looking for a good base for 21st Century politic, Jefferson's Bill for Establishing Religious Freedom and Madison's Memorial and Remonstrance are classic touchstones to which we can refer. Liberalism calls for freedom from religion, but also demands freedom for religion.

So, where and when did our problems start?

The great fracture in Western philosophy happened late 18th/early 19th century in a Europe that had become a cauldron of contradictions. The English Industrial Revolution, German philosophy, French Revolution mixed with colonialism, scientific discovery, rabid capitalism, and general social upheaval, creating fertile ground for the emergence of Friedrich Nietzsche. You might say: one more German philosopher, what's the big deal?

Well, Nietzsche developed a theory based on a total rejection of all Judeo-Christian values and that was and is a big deal. His wasn't a push to introduce modernity into Religious Theology; it was the pronouncement 'God is dead.'

One oddity of Nietzsche's writing is that his philosophy does not contain any system of thought. His work is brilliant and original and exists as a kind of deconstructionist grab bag for all. Some believe anybody can find something they like or hate. He is difficult for some because he wasn't afraid of contradictions. His main target was the values we live by and he was a very effective provocateur and powerful aphorist. Here are just a few: "morality is nothing other (therefore no more) than obedience to custom" or "There is no such thing as moral phenomena, but only an interpretation of phenomena..." and this "Virtue is still the most expensive vice: It should remain so!"

The Nazis used his claims to justify their racial theories; 70 million corpses later, we know where that ended. Perhaps Nietzsche predicted this misuse of his work, when he wrote that "The pigs will wallow in my theories." ['Anonymous' own translation from German] He also wrote on a wide variety of other subjects, including art, gender and many others: "In revenge and in love women are more barbaric than men". To which one might reply: see Othello, men can be just as barbaric!

But here we are especially interested in the part of his work that relates to social values. Nietzsche had a visceral hatred of Judeo-Christian values. His anti-philosophy was attractive to many, not only the Nazis. Many formidable intellectuals who could use such a "tabula rasa" to build their own, free of any constraint, were very influenced by Nietzsche.

The big Nazi swine died in Hitler's Berlin bunker in 1945 but many little swine survived. Martin Heidegger, Nietzsche's primary heir, took over the responsibility of adapting the destruction of Judeo-Christian values into the modern world. His philosophical theories became the foundation of Fascism and Nazism. The Democratic/Liberal values system was anathema to the Nazis. Heidegger was a pure product of Germany's right-wing intelligentsia who did not digest their World War I defeat (1918). He sought to use the Nietzschean's critic of Judeo-Christianity to justify the implementation of Fascism in Germany.

In 1926, well before Hitler's rise, Heidegger was already active with the most reactionary wing of the German right. He was a supporter of Rohm's SA, small army of right-wing thugs, and was greatly disappointed when Hitler, chose to have them exterminated, and replaced by the SS, another army of thugs but pure Nazis. It's like being dismayed that Hitler chose cholera over plague! Heidegger was involved politically with fascism until 1945. A due paying member to the end; he was the house intellectual philosopher of the Nazis.

Before his death in 1976 he had ample time to influence some European philosophers, French especially who minimized his Nazi past and thought it extraneous to his philosophical work. We beg to differ. The Nazi theories are inextricably linked to his philosophical work. Fortunately, most French philosophers kept their distance. A few involved in Postmodernism, especially the deconstructionists, which all, to a greater or lesser extent, were attracted to and influenced by

Heidegger's work. The not-so-funny part of that story is that all those philosophers were hyper-intellectuals but were writing about theories deeply anti-intellectual. They hated reason, rationality, normality, etc. The case of Michel Foucault is extreme. In the conclusion of his book *Madness and Civilization* he upholds the "sovereign enterprise of unreason"!

Concomitant to World War II, postmodernism emerged as an intellectual reaction against the certitude of sciences and rationality. It was based mainly in all form of arts but also in philosophy. While a tenet of modernism is the belief in 'universal truth', the central tenet of Postmodernism, is the concept of 'cultural relativism'. The grotesque transgressions of WWII, were also at the heart of deconstructionism and post- structuralism and subsets of post-modernism. When it spread to the U.S. it had a very different impact than in Europe. If it had remained in academia everything would have been fine but militants from some Humanities Department chose to bring that culture to the American people. The transplant didn't work. American masses aren't about sophisticated intellectual games. It's about business, sports and churches, and we are very good at it. But some people from the humanities didn't intend to let it go. They wanted to make homosexuality, radical feminism, radical minorities, racism, etc. their Vietnam War. They just forgot we lost that one!

It is a tricky intellectual and social business to move sophisticated ideas from academia to the masses. Especially when the strong set of stabilizing and unifying set of social values, is totally disregarded by one side, as it was by so many in the '70/'80s left. Bad-Academia was blindsided by its own pretension and arrogance. Their ideas, misinterpreted by militants from a myriad of political sub-groups, were reduced to sound bites by the media, and had catastrophic consequences on our society. When we read that women need men like a fish need a bicycle that is funny; when we read that all sex is rape, that is catastrophic.

Some of those intellectual extremists are now the laughingstock, not only of the public, but also from serious academia. It is so bad that people from higher education are thinking about suppressing tenure, which is a job guarantee for life. Peggy McIntosh's garrulous 'Daily Effects of white privilege' (csusm.edu), is an example of why life-long appointees can be useless and end up in the 'twilight zone.'

You need to be politically savvy with the help of a strong organization, to execute the conversion between ideas and action. If you have not achieved this, any intellectual proposal will crumble because of the lack of a centrifugal force to keep the theory unified. Ideology is the bridge between reality as it is and the world as we want it to be. If there is no social contract with solid values to fuse those ideas from academia, and make them acceptable for the society in general, they will disintegrate into a multitude of tiny fragments, grasped by groups of militants more dogmatic than the previous ones. The absurd mediocrity of our political debates probably derives from there.

We want to make sure that the readers don't interpret our criticism of some academics as a condemnation of academia--far from it. Our opinion of academia? Very simple: Viva Academia! Thank you to all thinkers, researchers, biologists, physicists, chemists, brainiacs of all kinds. But also thank you to all the ones working in the humanities, the philosophers, the linguists, the musicians, from religious studies to history, who make all of us a little bit less ignorant. You see, we are big fans of academia. But it won't stop us from criticizing the group of academics involved in human sciences which have a devastating influence on our society.

Heidegger's work was a big help at critiquing our value system that the post-modernists so despise. The deconstruction of our civilization has been going on for over 50 years and we see the results now. To criticize the excesses of the West is totally justified; but sadly, the deconstructionists threw the baby out with the dirty water. So, what do we have instead? Not much, people, not much.

The RRMs want to convince us that subjectivism, consumerism, homosexuality, moral relativism, updated racism, nihilism, alternate facts, etc. must be our new values, because courage, patriotism, honesty, generosity, effort, and tolerance are too old and decrepit. Well, it is a problem for us, because we think what they call their values are just the resultant product of a culture, where buckets full of opinions, half-baked theories, and an inordinate number of feelings, political manipulations etc. are their new reality that the infosphere/media system is drilling into their brains. So, they ask us, not so politely, to get the 'f..k out of their way' with our cardinal virtues of prudence, justice, faith, fortitude, hope, charity, love. Their narcissism blinds them to the reality that our values were established by thousands and thousands of years of human experience.

The pretension, arrogance or just plain stupidity of those people is baffling. We could disregard them as just an expression of abuse of the first Amendment, so frequent in democracy, but we would be making a great mistake. They aren't attacking the most retrograde political aspects of our country; they are attacking the values sustaining democracy and humanism. We aren't witnessing the usual fight between our two conceptions of democracy, the Democrat and the Republican; it is a much deeper conflict at the level of what justifies democracy. Who is going to control it? For what purpose? What is the ultimate goal of the Badfem, the sexualists, radical racist minorities, infosphere/media complex and megaCorps?

It is what our book is about, trying to make simple a very complex chess game between different social groups. Our society doesn't look good unless you are a member of the 10% who don't give a hoot about the rest of us!

But why did it happen more in the US and less in Europe, which was the cradle of those ideas? You must know that in Europe, theories are "food for thought" for those long evenings, invariably around a dining table covered with great food and some excellent bottles of vine, with passionate conversations, sometimes brilliant, always noisy and at the end amiable. The Italian, German, Spanish, English, the French, etc. absorb those theories from their intellectuals with a grain of salt, because their school system can produce a lot of them which are in a constant competition at a high level of abstraction. It is part of their culture. Academia is integrated socially but somehow theories coming from it are seen just as what they are, theories.

Let's see, we have some information to give to our readers. We would like to start with a social movement call feminism.

FEMINISM

"Woman's virtue is man's greatest invention."
Cornelia Otis Skinner.

"The truth will set you free, but first it will piss
you off." Gloria Steinem (?)

"In the sex war, thoughtlessness is the weapon
of the male, vindictiveness of the female." Cyril
Connolly

"Once power was considered a masculine at-
tribute. In fact, power has no sex." Katharine
Graham

"Do you know that one of the great problems of
our age is that we are governed by people who care
more about feelings than they do about thoughts
and ideas." Margaret Thatcher

"We have a Bill of Rights. What we need is a bill of
responsibilities." Bill Maher

Disclosure: All political structures and theories are fair game for critique. A civilization which brought us two World Wars, the Holocaust, the Vietnam War, the de-industrialization of America, the Iraqi war deserves be criticized and judged by its citizens. The feminists certainly have the right to do it. But what the radical feminists didn't have the right to do was to lie, falsify facts, mislead women and men, and manufacture research for more than half a century. Actually, they just followed the steps of Joseph Goebbels, Hitler's Minister of Propaganda, who wrote "Truth was unimportant and entirely subordinate to tactics and psychology." In politics *"If you use the same tools as your opponents, you will share the consequences."* (USDF)

Brief, very brief overview of more than half a century of feminism. We won't be focusing on their theories per se. We focus more on our need to comprehend why we have so much, not feminism, but Bad-fem politics, at the highest level of our socio-political life. We must start from the origin of that movement and see how early on the political seed of dogmatism, manipulation, lies etc. became a permanent fixture of that movement.

When Taylor Swift said: "Feminism is another word for equality."

Hilary Clinton said: "A feminist is someone who believes in equal rights."

All men and women in our group, including most of the interviewees, agree on these sentiments. So, all of us who contributed to the book are good feminists. But it doesn't relieve us of the responsibility to exemplify why after half a century, things have gotten worse for all of us and we have some questions for the self-appointed leadership of the feminist movement.

We divided feminism in three groups.
Let's call the good feminism: Good-fem.
The so-so feminist: Soso-fem.
The bad feminist, Bad-fem.

It's not very sophisticated but it will be useful for this discussion. Within the spaces between these three categories there is a lot of middle of the road feminism. Of course, everyone has the right to express their opinion. But we never find agreement with Bad-fems since the impact of their ideas are catastrophic for women, and our goal is to let the reader see and understand the riptide underneath which 3rd Wave feminists are drowning. Why did this happen? What kind of wrong turns did feminism make to steer it into such brackish waters? Once, one of the most promising social movements of the Twentieth Century, what were the missteps that created such hapless and ignoble deterioration? We want to understand why feminism is under the control of bad feminism, the culprit behind these crimes. We don't have any obligation, whatsoever, to support their politic. The fourth, fifth etc. waves are just bromidic, see later our Addendum on what Intersectionality is. (see ADDENDUM)

WHEN, WHERE AND WHY FEMINISM

The feminist movement, first wave, was born in up-state New York, during Seneca's Convention of 1848. The second wave proceeded from the Civil Rights movement in the 1960s and was mainly an urban phenomenon. We certainly appreciate all the efforts and progress due to that period. Most baby-boomers were involved in it.

It started when upper middle class, well-educated women got bored to death staying at home. That's a fact! It didn't start with millions of women storming Capitol Hill, and burning the White House to the ground, screaming for revolution. It began in comfortable living rooms in houses outfitted with modern appliances. It was a movement of comfortable middle-class white women that introduced these brave new ideas to us. They were right to do so! It was the millions of newly educated women who would be poised to create more prosperity as well as prepared to contribute new ideas that would help us progress. But from the beginning, there was something afoul brewing from a minority of women militants. Those were frustrated by their inability to include their personal sexual political claims in the discourse of the general debate of the time. So, the third wave, 1990, emerged from the second one, carrying in it a worm who grew much bigger!

We are focusing on the third wave because it is the source of feminist problems. Instead of creating a fact and research-based series of positions that support their views, the most radical among them, the brick throwers if you will, chose the option of going all noise. Their tactics undermined their own objectives. They chose hysteria over careful argument and volume over substance. Why don't we understand more about women and men and their relation to power and sex? And, more important, why don't we have a deeper, wider and more profound understanding of what's going on between the sexes during this moment of seismic transformation in our society? There are so many questions we can't begin to analyze and answer thanks to the obfuscating Bad-fems who have choked to death any reasonable debate by their insistence on hyperbole and provocation instead of an honest and constructive conversation.

Why aren't feminists curious enough to study why men are the way they are? After all, they are claiming all over that only women raise children aren't they? So, what happened since sweet little boys end up, according to bad-fem, rapists, misogynists, violent, sexist pigs? What went wrong? Who made sweet little boys become these monsters? Can't we expect some explanation from the feminists' talking head? Well, keep waiting for any kind of explication which might have helped resolve some conflicts in the male/female conundrum. They will tell you that there is no need to study men since women know them. The fact is they have no idea who they are, how they operate, or how they understand the world. Bad-fem's doctrinaire pig-headedness limits progress and growth. What was lost in the Bad-fem shuffle is feminism, which was so important to all of us.

The radical feminist chooses to write about women who were absent in HIS-Story" – their new word for male controlled history -- and therefore felt compelled to write their own story, to give a voice to all those women, kept silent by 'patriarchy'. What they failed to recognize is that for a long period of time, those uneducated and illiterate underclass masses were unrepresented in history books. The nature of their lives was known to the educated class who lived close to them. But only the powerful, historically significant men and women were included in the written history. Elizabeth

I, Catherine the Great, Admiral Nelson, Napoleon, George Washington, Joan of Arc (who was an illiterate maid), etc.– all were subjects of recorded history.

But Bad-fem's work is a-historical on purpose. They write their own history books to sustain their opinions instead of doing the opposite, which is to use historical facts to build their theories. They didn't have any use for the standard of modern historical research tools, which include archaeology, statistics, demography, sociology, etc. History, when used by honest people, can be a very powerful tool to understand why the society we live in is the way it is. An example of ludicrous manipulation of history by Bad-fems is their use of patriarchy as a key element to justify their politic. (see ADDENDUM)

We will later see how often they rely on purely anecdotal evidence taken from literature, instead of analysis and objective study based on facts. They made political decisions that were destructive to their cause, at times casting men as women's enemy. They continue to distract us from the fact that the emerging generation of young men in the 1960s also took on the feminist cause. By the late 1960s, young men were engaged in a battle to end the Vietnam War, the Civil Rights movement, the sexual revolution. In other words, they were a progressive political force as much as the feminists. So, our question is why feminism decayed so fast as a travesty of itself?

THE NATIONAL ORGANIZATION FOR WOMEN'S STATEMENT OF PURPOSE

The NOW movement, founded in June 1966, had a statement of purpose.

"We reject the current assumptions that a man must carry the sole burden of supporting himself, his wife, his family, and that a woman is automatically entitled to life-long support by a man upon her marriage.... We believe that a true partnership between the sexes demands a different concept of marriage, an equitable sharing of the responsibilities of home and children and of economic burdens of their support. We believe that proper recognition should be given to the economic and social value of homemaking and child-care." Did we agree on that? Oh yes! Did we reach our goals? Hell no! The proof for us is that NOW went from 16 million adherents paying dues to 500,000.

Edith Wharton famously wrote "there are two ways of spreading light, one can be the candle or the mirror that reflects it." This is a perfect metaphor for the historic trajectory of feminism. The candle is original impulse and idea that gave birth to it, the mirror is the vehicle that reflects the candle's ideas and wishes. Well, in 2018, the mirror is a useless piece of crap and the candle has run its course and is dying. That movement is more than in bad shape. If we don't do something about it, it will be R.I.P. feminism very soon. It's already on life support.

Happily, there has been emerging recently a new line of thought from some feminists who have begun to see that serious trouble exists in the feminist movement. It's quite bad when women prefer to call themselves humanists, womanists, even manists! A lot of so-so feminists are expressing their discomfort with what feminism became. We certainly don't agree with all their conclusions, but our goal isn't to get into details regarding these. We just want to focus on the fact that women, and the American people in general, are paying the price of the sexist, sectarian, dogmatic Bad-fem's politic.

THE WORM IN THE APPLE:

Our readers have to remember a meaningful incident which happened in 1963. Some members of NOW organization sought Betty Friedan's support for a female bisexuality member of the board. Friedan was appalled by the fact that the private sexuality of a woman could be of any interest when working on social and political issues of the feminist movement. Right there, early on, the worm was embedded in the apple. From that point on, the overlapping confusion between privacy, especially private sexuality and public politics were constant. The movement did not maintain focus on the socio-economic needs of women; rather they became obsessed with the personal. What does the part time homosexuality of a woman have to do with establishing a health care mobile facility in all remote sparsely populated regions? Absolutely nothing!

Well, we still don't have any mobile healthcare, but for sure, we have a very well-organized nationwide support system for homosexuals. Because you see, Bad-fems, in alliance with the sexualists, and the RRM, didn't want women's issues "limited to the narrow needs of women." The thought that assisting someone in becoming a healthy, well-educated, productive citizen could be interpreted or construed as a narrow issue is extraordinary. That it takes a quarter of our lives to obtain such a result and have a certain former presidential candidate berate us for "baking cookies," is to quote that candidate, again "deplorable."

What is the reason some educated feminist women end up being such a bunch of narrow-minded militants promoting ideas harmful to women? The answer is: education does not equal intelligence. You may have earned a degree from Barnard, Wellesley, Oberlin, Mount Holyoke or Smith, and still be out of touch. For them, knowledge, action and consequences are not linked together, and so we face possible disaster. All philosophical works from Descartes to Hegel show that when culture/education is coupled with thought/intelligence, it is a feast--one where they are never invited! But when it is not, when our will overtakes our careful thinking, we create confusion and distortions born of dogmatism. There is no bottom to how low humanity can sink. (see ADDENDUM)

WHAT IS FEMINISM?

We asked members of our group to find a good and clear definition of feminism. They could not come up with an accurate one! They chalked their failure up to the complexity of the issue. It has grown so complex that some Bad-fems claim that there are feminist interpretations of mathematics and physics! So, they must be in favor of Heisenberg's Uncertain Principle definition of Quantum Mechanics; since the particles "form a world of potentiality or possibilities rather than one thing of facts." Which is the exact definition of feminism that we see below.

In *What Is Feminism* a valuable book by Chris Beasley she writes, "In the main, feminists are inclined, frequently deliberately, not to define what they mean by feminism, sensing dangers such as internal policing of both the field and of feminists by those who might like to determine what is to be included (or not) as well as the potential danger of constricting the unstable vitality of its meaning....it leaves implicit definition.....fluid and extensive.... ".[1] The author offers here an excellent description of how feminists see themselves, but along with it, we can see how it shapes their politics.

That is a great way to let anybody think they can be feminist and open the door to anyone, including some quacks, who will bring their own agenda. It is that amorphous definition of feminism which is the cause number one of its failure. It is imperative for any socio-political movement to 'constrict the stable vitality of its meaning'; otherwise you will end up with a medley of divided groups unable to understand that *"Feminism will triumph only with men because if men are the problem, they are also the solution; and since we are equal, if men think women are the problem, they also are the solution."* (USDF)

C. Beasley gives us a quick enumeration of the sub-branches of feminism, which are liberal, poststructuralist, radical, Lacanian, genderist, Marxist, lesbian, cultural, black, eco-feminists, New Age feminists, radical, i-feminist etc. (ibid p. 46) On our side we found male feminists and male feminist lesbians! (we aren't making those up!) Gee, that's a lot of options for any woman to choose from. So, when a woman says, I am a feminist, we must ask her: What kind of feminist are you? and that, in view of the fact that it is extremely convenient for them and their movement to remain vague about what it really is. All of them can say: we are good people on the side of victim. But if they are radical gender feminists and hate half the population of this country, they are not good people, they are political opportunists, gender racist pigs, who are using feminism for their own purposes. Alas, feminism is now just a big tent plenty of people live under and use it for their own ambitions. Are they good squatters who have a positive impact on feminism or are they just vampires sucking its blood? We need to know. But our group believes that it isn't the responsibility of men to clean up that mess, but ours, women who used to have a decent political movement.

It must be done, because we know that Donald Trump is president in large part due to the failure of the Bad-fem's politic, who were 100% behind Hilary Clinton's candidacy. Is it where half a century of feminism was supposed to end? Let's look in detail at their policies and its consequences on our society.

HOW BAD IS BAD-FEM INTELLECTUAL ACHIEVEMENT?

We have a lot of excellent books written by numerous intelligent, honest feminists available to us. But here we must stay focused on the Bad-fems because it is important to show how dishonest and deceitful their work is. To grasp the extent of the manipulations let's look at what Christina Hoff Sommers wrote about three decades ago.[4] She is an equity feminist, who has debunked lies and manipulations by the likes of Gloria Steinem who in *The Revolution from Within* book, informed her readers that "in this country alone...about 150,000 females die of anorexia each year." Steinem quoted Naomi Wolf's, *The Beauty Myth,* who was herself referencing to *Fasting Girls, the Emergence of Anorexia Nervosa as a modern*

Disease, by Joan Brumberg, former director of Women's Studies at Cornell University. She in turn attributes the figure to the American Anorexia and Bulimia Association. So, Cristina Hoff-Sommers called Dr. Diane McKinley, the president's association, who said "We were misquoted"! The newsletter referred to 150,000 to 200,000 sufferers of anorexia. What was the correct mortality rate? Between 100 to 400 deaths a year, was the real number. It is unbelievable that an academic director from Cornell University points out that women who study eating problems, don't even try to understand a problem but "seek to demonstrate that "...these disorders are an inevitable consequence of a misogynistic society that demeans women...by objectifying their bodies." This is one sample of where and when Badfem thrust the word misogyny as an established academic fact in our social discourse.

Not one among all of them, at the highest level of academia, did the basic fact-checking on such a claim, not one. They weren't seeking facts, they just wanted to build their theory on opinions, prejudice, feelings, etc. with fake facts! From the beginning the Badfem used any kind of quackery and intellectual rip offs, because "A lie told once remains a lie, but a lie told a thousand times become the truth." -Joseph Goebbels apparently was inspired by Lenin's "A lie told often becomes the truth."

The quotes above from Hoff-Sommers are from 25 years ago. Let's see if something changed.

In September 21, 2015, The New York Times had a dramatic headline: "1 in 4 Women Experience Sex Assault on Campus." Well, that was unacceptable. Knowing the pernicious effect of Bad-fem's propaganda, we started to pay attention to the news. We were right because the authors of the 288-page report complained several times publicly, that this was a misleading reading of their work. Did the NYT correct the published articles? Did they give a courtesy call to the researchers? Did they do some basic fact-checking? Did it apologize to their readers? No, they didn't, and the result is millions and millions of people on our side believed that story and were appalled by that atrocious comportment of male students in our universities. The fact is that, according to the statistics of the DOJ, there are less cases of rape on campus that in the general population! A more accurate front page of the NYT should have been Brian D. Earp's. "Approximately 1 in 4 of 19% of a non-representative sample of women who responded to a non-representative sample survey of 27 colleges (out of roughly 5,000) reported experiencing sexual assault, where 'sexual assault' is taken to mean anything from being on the receiving end of an unsolicited kiss to forcible penetration at gunpoint, regardless of the particular context."

That kind of deception has consequences. Researchers must now not only correct the information carried by media but refrain from publishing the results of some studies. They are afraid it will be exploited politically by any media whore in need of news to fill out their megaphone.[2]

Bad-Academics could be just a bunch of annoying talking heads. But medias give legitimacy to any kind of ideas, by massively diffusing them. Some create in the public those absurd and dangerous convictions based on nothing more than hypothesis. It holds meaning not only for those who believe in them but the general public which have no reason, time, knowledge to probe and investigate what is in their newspaper, TV news, etc. It is the responsibility of the media to do it. But they removed the crucial safety gate of fact-checking on most socio-political issues. So, anything goes! We see here a disturbing collusion between the Bad-fems, Bad-academia and media. If we look at the NYT, our newspaper, can we ask if there is any body around Mr. Sulzberger, looking for quackery, ridiculous affirmations? In the infosphere/media chapter we develop those issues in depth.

Mr. Shulzberger is not the only one responsible for the progressive quality reduction of articles in The New York Times; the tenor of the paper seems to have changed from journalists reporting the news, to journalists opining about the news (see 'Taking a Stand Against an Employer. NYT, June 14, 2020) We read in "Taking a Stand Against an Employer" (the NYT, Sunday, June 14, 2020) because the journalist found "deeply appalling" an Op-Ed by Senator Tom Cotton published by her newspaper and went on berating her bosses for letting us read it This is just baffling to us. Someone must explain that the readers have a brain of their own and can read an opinion piece without having a journalist explaining to them (us) the meaning of it. To call fascism anything she disagrees with won't do for us. We welcome open dialogue with people who don't share our opinions. It is an abomination to her that we start a dialogue, see how many concerns we have in common, and try to resolve even the smallest issues. We applaud those women from Pro-Life and Pro-Choice who put together some successful bills to improve the situation of working women in their State. We don't have any confidence in some journalists who want to censure us because we determine to use our mind. Our question to them is: "Who do those bad journalists, think they are?" (See chapter Infosphere/ media were we broaden that issue)

It is the lack of oversight by people in charge of information which creates such a distortion, a disconnection from reality that breeds deception and trickery. Let's see another sample of our being grossly manipulated: between 300,000 to1,000,000 girls are pressed into sexual slavery each year in the United States. What a juicy number for the media! In fact, those numbers are referring to children in possible danger of exploitation, not actual victims. The research team of Richard Estes and Neil Alan Weiner, when interviewed by Village Voice about those numbers, said: "We are talking about of few hundred people," and "Those that are actually abducted and pressed into slavery include many boys." A New York City 2008 census shows that half of all underage prostitutes are boys. It is inadmissible that young girls can be reduced to it. Why does Badfem never recognize the horrible life of boys in the same situation? Certainly not. Do those boys just get what they deserve? Some of the interviewees, when aware of the disdain, coldness, disinterest of those Radfems about the life of boy victims of sexual abuses, called them 'feminist turds.'

We could think of all people using 'victim feminism' as bigoted idiots. (See the one clowning around with her mattress in Columbia University.) But we would be making a grave mistake because they use the "victim" concept to eviscerate any discourse about progress done, so they always must overbid themselves with more and more--from freakish to nonsensical--claims. For Badfem, women's situation was horrible before and now it is worse. And they refuse to acknowledge that since they are self-appointing themselves as the leaders, they are responsible for it. Before you read something about women who aren't unidimensional, we would like to mention a movement we welcome and supported for a while.

FROM @METOO TO TIME'S UP

Even with the best intentions a movement like Time's Up can't bring any lasting solution; because politically it couldn't convert itself into a coherent socio-political program.

It wasn't easy to topple people like Harvey Weinstein, well safeguarded as he was, by his talent as a high-powered movie producer, who play a major financial role in Hollywood, in addition to propelling many actresses to stardom. For the same reasons, however, enable him to act in unconscionable ways with women who have accused him of forcing himself on them.

He was resentful toward the one who refused his advances by limiting the careers of Ashley Judd and Mira Sorvino. The moral corruption of Hollywood's culture forms the background of that kind of abuse. So, we are grateful to #MeToo and Time's Up for exposing the madness. But sending Harvey Weinstein and a few other to jail isn't enough. Nothing is truly resolved by this, considering that he is a product of a culture which prevails throughout our society.

The first difficulty is the total absence of a definition of sexual abuse. #MeToo is a collection of complaints about men from any woman out there. In that wide array you can find everything from real horror stories, to made up ones. Rape isn't a female delusion, so it was Time's

Up responsibility to work on the cases of real sexual abuses and make clear that they rejected the ridiculous ones. If you don't, you are responsible for all the crazy stories from #MeToo!

Tarana Burke, Oprah Winfrey, Alyssa Milano, etc. should have been, on such an issue, all over the media to defend the 'due process' just to make sure they were targeting the right people. They didn't because they think that their celebrity gives them credibility, some insight, into any kind of problems. Well, they can be a billionaires, a talented actresses and not be competent enough to handle a socio-cultural issue which are totally foreign to their expertise. If it did, they would have made clear to Mean Girls of any high schools, that it isn't acceptable to use sexual abuse to gang up against a teenage boy. That a woman can't consider as domestic abuse the slamming of a door by a man on his way out of an argument. Time's Up didn't tell Bad-fems to shut up, instead of blaming a man who was innocent of an accusation of rape, it came from a woman who just wanted attention. He dared to claim his innocence, but they wouldn't accept this because it was "detrimental to the cause of women".

We already wrote that we supported that movement because there are some bad people out there: pedophiles, abusers, rapists, etc. and we want to get rid of them. But Time's Up made the same mistakes as feminism. It was never able to reject absurd claims made by one of the wackiest accusers. Most people, and we are among them, want to be associated with responsible people, not crackpots, since they bring confusion, skepticism, incoherence and make it impossible to know the truth. Do we all have the obligation now to accept as true what

Jackie from UVA.? or Crystal from Duke University are saying because we must always 'believe women'? And what about all the Hollywood's Ambers? The Roses? The Karens? Etc.

As for us, we can be revolted by gross injustice and at the same time be aware that education, intelligent laws, etc. will be the way to resolve our problems. What won't work is the hysteria pushed everywhere in our society by Badfem. It will end up destroying not only #MeToo but Time's Up which will lose all credibility considering that nobody will believe their claims, especially men.

"Everybody is entitled to their opinion on the male gender but show them how smart you are by not thinking they are all stupid." (USDF)

If we don't look at social problems in their context, we won't be able to resolve any of them. For example, sexuality and violence are everywhere. A good start would be to look where it is, and who brought it there. If we want to live in a decent society, we must make those people aware of the fact that we are tired of some of their achievements. We don't have a problem with business media; but we certainly do have one with their apathy for some of their productions which are abhorrent, shameful and so vicious that we are convinced now that it isn't by accident that they put it on the market. It is too systematic. It fits too well the purpose of a culture of "anything goes" implemented by people who gain something from it, mainly $. In infosphere/media we develop at length our concern about it.

WOMEN AREN'T UNIDIMENSIONAL

It is a given that all reasonable people can accept that women are not one-dimensional. The Christian veil of white gauze with shimmering pink covering the female gender for centuries is gone. Gone also are the myths of moral superiority, unselfishness and maternal love packed into the notion of women as 'Mother of God'. These have been effective tropes helping to install women to an elevated place in Western Society. However, the pedestal was far too high for the feminists, who saw its placement as progenitor of women's powerlessness. It must be destroyed. But when you remove something it has to be replaced with something else. Otherwise you are just creating a hole and weakening the social fabric.

So, what could be the energizing principle to fill that hole? Solidarity among women, wondered Badfem? They absolutely wanted to get rid of that 'Mother of God' stuff! Why not make them victims!! TADA! They found their motherlode! It's now the synthesis of all feminist theory: victims of misogyny, of their boyfriends, victims of history, victims of sexism, victims of gender, victim of their boss, victim of childbirth, victims of their own sex, victims of their neighbors, husbands etc. Victim, victim, victim.

Does sexism exist? Yes, it does! Does misogyny exist? Yes, it does! Does domestic violence exist? Yes, it does! But for our Badfem, being a victim is the constant unceasing dominant theme in the history of women. Before the '60s women couldn't, like men, be a product of their time. Women were so defective intellectually that they never understood, through millenniums, their condition.

It is important to say here that victimhood isn't a new feminist theory per se but an outcome of Bad-feminist posturing. But, unfortunately for women, that kind of noisy hectoring, drowning out the Goodfem, went viral in our society. There is no more feminism theory; there is only a victim theory, with its corollary entitlement. If you are a victim, you are entitled to compensation!

Goodfem take responsibility. They will tell you that they know exactly what they are doing, getting, or giving during oral sex. One interviewee, a 35-year-old woman said, "There is no confusion for us women, we know when our body tells us we need sex. Our brain may tell us that we could find a better mate than the one next to us, but we chose to have sex anyway and we take responsibility for our choices. We don't need recovered memory therapy to reinterpret what we were doing fifteen years ago with our male partner! What you (meaning the interviewer) call Bad-fems assumes we are all a bunch of brainless morons!" It assumes that a woman is so pathetically weak, that she can't have sex without coercion. Obviously, Bad-fems cannot face the fact that WOMEN CAN BE violent, vulgar, cruel, vicious, liars, cheaters, manipulative, delusional, confused, conspiratorial, sadistic, abusive, thieves, nymphomaniacs, dishonest, hysterical, lazy, vain, murderers, opportunists, gossips and as stupid AS MEN CAN BE. And men can be courageous, collaborative, persuasive, strong, generous, kind, honest, heroic, empathic, loving husband and father, intuitive, creative, passionate, life-long learners, good listeners, responsible, good leaders and as intelligent AS WOMEN CAN BE.

This is where the equality between women and men

rests, at the roots of what it means to be human. Sorry if you are disappointed; but women and men must deal with and accept that reality, or there will be no equality between them. Many women and men understand it, but this simple fact seems to elude Bad-fems! The needs of human society are the primary driving force behind the division of labor. *"Obviously one person can't perform all needed functions and sometimes those divisions are separated by gender. For example, men go to war and get killed and women make babies to replace them. If you are a Baby boomer, woman or man, you are a result of that division of labor."* (USDF) (see ADDENDUM)

LET'S GO BACK TO OUR BADFEM

Most theorical and political work done by Badfem are undermined by dogmatism.

There is a long tradition of political narrow mindedness and ideological dogmatism in feminism. If we look at the suffragettes, Prohibition, the E.R.A., intolerance and rigidity, is rampant. A sample of it is Prohibition. It was a response to the problem of alcoholism and prostitution in large cities. After the downfall of the original Suffragists movement in the1900, which focused on reforming the political apparatus, the more militant members of the suffragettes movement took over the Temperance Movement with such dogmatism and self-righteousness, that their politic ended up as the catastrophic Volstead Act, more commonly known as "Prohibition". It encouraged the criminal side of capitalism by letting gangsters run a huge black-market economy. That one, in the '20s to '30s, was the size of the illegal drug problem in today's economy. *"Ideological dogmatism, that they confuse with political assertiveness, was the primary failure of Prohibition, like today it explains Bad-feminism failure."* (USDF)

BADFEM'S POLITIC CORRUPT DEMOCRACY

Let's see a sample of how Bad-fems theories pervert democracy. Russlynn Ali, an assistant secretary for the office of civil rights at the Department of Education, sent an official policy letter to colleges and universities around the country. In that letter, sent without any supervision from the Senate, lawyers from Congress etc., she didn't use the standard protocol of asking for 'answers and comments', which such documents usually require, since it gives to the recipient the opportunity to respond with comments that could be incorporated in the refinement of the final policy. By not doing this, Ali's office was threatening colleges and universities with having their Federal funding revoked if they did not follow her new directives. Who and how many employees are on the pay roll of our administration, who avail themselves to change drastically the rules, the norms of our society, according to their political opinions? We need to know; in one of our future books we will look at it in detail.[3]

Of course, colleges depend on funding and are inclined to do whatever is necessary to preserve that source of income in order to survive, even if it means sacrificing students to protect their financial assistance. They rushed to implement these Title IX recommendations. The result was that universities opened kangaroo courts run by people with no training or knowledge in handling criminal cases of sexual assault and rape. In these courts, a defendant does not have access to a lawyer and cannot confront their accuser etc. The consequences for the accused are potentially dire: expulsion and a stain on the person's record for life, if it isn't long term jail time and all that could be done anonymously. (*Not anymore, thanks to a Republican, Mrs. De Vos, Secretary of Education!*)

Any fruitcake or dingbat under the influence of any kind of drugs, alcohol or not, can accuse anybody of anything. At the same time, we have horrible things that actually do happen: real rapes, domestic violence, murders, and we must listen, spend money, etc. because some narcissist imbeciles decide to mobilize the police, the press and everybody must be concerned by their made-up fantasies. *"Bad-fems aren't hysterics but are expert at creating hysteria and use it as a political tool to advance their politic. Their main tools are researches, studies, statistics from Bad-academia or not, that they will manipulate to the extent of making it fit their claims."* (USDF)

When radical feminists actively try to remove the "due process" from any judicial decision concerning women we must remind them that due process is imbedded in the 14th Amendment. It hails as far back as the Magna Carta, the foundational document of human rights signed in the late 13th century. *"Due process is part of the law of the Land as well as Habeas Corpus. These are the bedrock of Western Civilization, of our notion of liberty. Let's be clear, we will not accept a removal of any part of it from our Judicial System."* (USDF)

What is appalling to us is that it happened during Obama's Administration. This is shocking! It is our political side which is wreaking havoc on the foundation of democracy! If a woman is a victim of sexual aggression or a rape, which is a crime, and refuses to go through the judicial system, what is the validity of her claim? It is the Badfem who removed 'sexual misconduct,' which goes from a student 'mooning' at a police car, to a woman showing her breasts from the balcony of her dorm to a bunch of noisy guys. All those incidents could be handled by a university board. Not anymore--now, anything happening to a woman is a crime no matter what, no matter where, no matter how ridiculous the claim is. If there is a crime, the judicial system must be involved, but who is against it? The Bad-fems, who wants a 'special jurisdiction' to handle their matters where the due process won't exist anymore since we "must believe all women." So, in 'the future is women.' we won't have the right to a lawyer to defend ourselves? Well, their future looks like the past, straight out of the Dark Middle-Ages.

How far can that kind of stinky ideology pervade our Academia? Well, Neera Tenden said "guilty people obstruct, innocent people cooperate." She has a Juris Doctor degree from Yale where she was submissions editor & policy review. So, when you are accused of anything if you hire a lawyer who is going to 'obstruct' any accusation, since it's his job, is the proof for her that you are guilty! People like her can't work in any judicial system based on 'innocent until proven guilty'. Her quote reflects how she thinks, how her brain processes guilt and innocence. These kinds of people are incredibly dangerous for democracy since they bring progressively the concept of you are 'guilty until proven innocent' into the judicial system.[5]

TOXIC FEMINITY Vs.
TOXIC MASCULINITY

When people say that toxic feminism exists, Badfem is up in arms, claiming that it is a false equivalence established by male militants. They are wrong. Bad feminism is toxic. Let's give two examples.

What happens when a woman pops three ecstasy, drinks five shots of tequila, several beers, a few uppers and goes home with a man where they have sex, and then claims in the morning that she has been raped, because she can't remember if she gave him the right type of consent or not. It is a scandal with catastrophic social consequences! Thanks to the culture of victimhood, she can be in denial of two tied-up fundamentals in a democracy: freedom *and* responsibility. But she will find plenty of support from the 'don't blame the victim' movement, which ends up infantilizing women instead of empowering them, by making them not responsible for any of their actions. The problem is that some women are not victims, but pleasure seekers who think the highest good in life is hedonism. So, don't talk about responsibility with such as her. Talk self-indulgence and depravity; she is in pursuit of her pleasure only. The Radfem think that false accusations of rape are just incidentals, outliers. They are dead wrong! It's just the tip of the iceberg! Many young men are now embroiled in a variation on the same theme: young women who are unable to handle the responsibility that their sexual freedom required are blaming men. This is what we mean by toxic femininity. It is now, like toxic masculinity, everywhere in our culture.

The other example is when boys, even the little ones, are in school they can be victims of discrimination by female teachers who refuse to involve them in the Q and A of the class. Those teachers push girls to the detriment of boys, since they see them as future incestuous patriarch, rapists, misogynists, sexist pigs. Boys are victim of the vicious Bad-fems' culture of 'it is payback time for men'. They gloat in the idea let's screw the education of their sons and put girls in charge. Please be aware that we did not aggrandize those examples. They are now basic facts of our social life. Our educational system has too many of those women and men totally under the incantation of a half century of Bad-fem propaganda. Boys bad, Girls good dichotomy is totally ingested. It is unacceptable to the point that some people are asking now to reopen schools for girls and for boys separately.

On a lighter side: we found in geekfeminism.com the following: "... toxic masculinity enables abuses... toxic feminism doesn't exist but is benevolent sexism." Everybody in our group couldn't stop laughing when reading it. Those Bad-fems can be a riot when they want to be. If Wikipedia expects to keep some credibility it must turn down any editing done by groups of people with an agenda; like those Bad-feminist professors who put several dozen students working on editing every article written on women's issues. (see by Talia Lavin, Feminist Edit-A-thon seeks to reshape Wikipedia, The New Yorker, March 11, 2016. Also see: geekfeminism. com}. We have too many examples of how the so-called research studies from Bad-fems politically manipulated trash for media consumption are.

BADFEM AND PRIVACY

The catastrophic consequences of the destruction of privacy.

The destruction of privacy is one determining factor which made possible the strike against women's abortion rights. It rested on two major Supreme Court decisions, Griswold Vs. Connecticut and Roe Vs. Wade, both based on women's right to privacy. That privacy was nested legally in her/his home. But our Bad-fems clamored all over the media that privacy was just hiding male domination and that privacy shouldn't exist in family but politics. By doing it, they removed the legal justification of women's rights to abortion since privacy was politic. All people against abortion rushed into it and used politics to chip away the rights to abortion! Why shouldn't they since imbecile-fems give them the opportunity to do it? We hope that our readers understand why we don't have any more patience for those people.

Naturally they appointed themselves to give us women an inordinate number of opinions on how we must handle our orgasms, - remember the G. Spot! – the right way to comprehend abortion, to grasp the meaning of our hidden homosexuality, to decipher heterosexuality, to interpret housework, to make sense of volunteer activities, to perceive the significance of aging, to get a drift at what a rape really is, we shouldn't forget that being a homemaker is worse than Stalin's gulags and motherhood is the ultimate expression of female stupidity and male dominance. We had to endure, for half a century, their lectures and homilies about a revolution which never happened. Instead we got from them dogmatism, disorganization, confusion, idiocy, hostility, mob rule etc.

They are just intelligent enough to classify all chores around the house done by men, changing car oil, mowing the lawn, cleaning gutters, fixing electrical problems, and some are competent enough to replace a boiler, fix a roof, under "Hobby" when it occurs! That way, men's work doesn't appear in any of their statistics and it is the proof for Badfem that they never participate in domestic chores. Is it just an innocuous matter? No, it is not, it is a poison in any relationship, because women think they are exploited by men who think they aren't valued.

We will always deny the right to the government, to law enforcement, to our churches, etc. to encroach on our private lives. We have laws which prevent interference from any groups that attempt to assert their moral authority over the general population. Why do they think we should let them do it with our lives? We have the right to participate in any group that fills our emotional or spiritual needs. The arts that we see, the charities we give to, the books we want to read, etc.–all these are private decisions. The Bad-fems are the ones who originated the destruction of privacy. They opened the door, thirty years ago, to the infosphere/media onslaught on our private lives. In another chapter we will see the consequences of their socio-political incompetence. Remember, our book is about bad feminism, not the good kind!

THE CRADLE OF BADFEM'S THEORIES IS IN BADACADEMIA

So, let's start with the head of their movement because, as the Chinese say, a fish rots from the head down. We again must confirm that we respect and need academia and we want to make sure nobody is confused between the bad fringe of human science, which has the proclivity of publishing from wacky to preposterous theories, and the rest of a great institution called academia. It is where most critical research occurs. Some research that proves unhelpful, is of course, all part of the process of trial and error which is essential to a line of inquiry. When research remains true to the values of rationality and established scientific method it can go an enormous distance, even to the planet Mars. Some theories rooted in quackery will pop up from time to time in academia. The Kinsey Report on human sexuality is an example of this. (We aren't writing about the Kinsey institute, which is a time-honored research establishment.) The key question is always to ask: Is the research rational and scientific? All studies based on anything other than a scientific approach must be examined carefully. Unfortunately, some positions lay claim to a foundation based on objective study but are instead based on feelings, opinions, and politics instead of objective inquiry; these can be useless and dangerous.

Many people carry around viewpoints from grade school through college. Teaching positions are especially vulnerable to that kind of abuse, especially the teaching of women's studies which has morphed into feminist studies in some colleges. Regrettably, some of those professors just come in with their opinion and teach it. This is not education but indoctrination, and it is where most academic propagandists are roosting. The first victims are young students who emerge from these courses thinking they know something when in fact the only thing they learn is the opinion of a teacher. But to learn an opinion results in a form of intellectual inertia. What you know has been already pre-digested intellectually; students don't need to go through their own mental process of analyzing, understanding, criticizing facts. They become just parrots who can't do any original research, not because they aren't intelligent but because they don't have the tools to do that critical job. [6] It is probably one more explanation for the general intellectual mediocrity of Bad-feminism which was able to come up with a cartoon character, Wonder Woman, as the UN Honorary ambassador for women. We must take back our feminism from those morons.

LET'S LOOK AT "VICTIMHOOD"

A talented actress got a small salary for a job when her male co-star made over $1.5 million for the same job. Nothing wrong with this. The man brings billions of dollars to the studio. The actress, more into artsy films, doesn't generate the same dollars. This is a business! So, when her co-star, with William Morris Agency, gave a total of $2,000,000 to Time's Up, because he feels guilty that he was paid more than her, that's the wrong answer. He makes it seem as if he has done something wrong, but he has not. Since when is it the responsibility of a man, in 2017, to care for the paycheck of his female co-worker? It is her responsibility, and hers only, to make sure that she gets what's owed to her. That actress was never a 'victim' of men. She never said she was, but Crappy-fem certainly did it for her all over the media.

Now, a corporation doesn't have the obligation to let people who work for it know that it is the under the control of some cheap CFO! The issue was with the finance department of that corporation, not American men as the Bad-fem clarion. 'Victimhood culture' has a reverse effect on the equality we try to establish. *"The Bad feminism politic consists of never working on the cause of an issue, but to always stay safely on the rich grassland of consequences, which are only a byproduct of the causes."* (USDF) Why? Because it is unsafe for them to work on, to fight the causes and take on powerful economic interests since they are on their 'media payroll'. Criticize that corporation, a heavyweight in that business and it will find a way to stop anybody carrying your messages. It will be a death sentence for Bad-fems which exists only thanks to the noise machine of those media corporations.

Another example: A SoSo-fem, Nancy Jo Sales' excellent book, (*American Girls, Social Media and the Secret Lives of Teenagers,* Vintage Books, NY,2017), shows us the profoundly negative impact of the media's culture on our youth. We were impressed. One of us spoke to her and asked when she was going to write the same book on American boys, because if girls must deal with "fuckboys" then boys have to confront "fuckgirls," don't they? Her answer was: "Never will I write such a book," meaning that only girls are victims. This is unfortunate because she leaves her readers uninformed about what boys are facing. She refuses to see that both boys and girls wrestle with societal expectations. Her narrow-minded feminism blinds her to the tragic reality that four times more boys kill themselves than girls and that there are as many boy prostitutes as girls.

Aren't we going too far? Well, the reverberation of their culture in our school system made someone send a 6-year-old little boy, who during recess dared to kiss the hand of a little girl, to the principal's office for sexual abuse accusations! This is how absurd the situation has become in America. That kind of story can exist only in a context where there is a total absence of measure, fairness, restraint, balance and a basic understanding of what a human society is.

A lot of people understand that if we take away from Badfems 'victimhood' from their arsenal of ideas, their argument system will collapse. They would have to acknowledge that their theories overall have a very negative effect on women who are supposed to be the big winners of half a century of their kind of feminism. The CDC recently published a report claiming, "drug overdose death rates in women in the United States have increased 260% in the past two decades…", from age 30 to 64. It is an increase of 13% a year. No wonder why Badfems prefer to talk about victimhood, patriarchy, sexism, misogyny etc. instead of knowing why women are nearly twice as likely as men to take anti-depressants (16% to 9% for men).

LET'S GO BACK TO "OUR SLUT"

Because she is a negative personage in any society, call her what you will: tramp, tart, Trollope, we have a bevy of names to call her. There are women who conspire to get pregnant with men because of the size of their bank account. There are others who want to destroy a couple by sleeping with one of the partners and making sure that the other knows it. And don't forget the ones who thrive on spreading lies about other women, etc. *"Most people believe the slut is alive and well, she exists, and we intend to keep shaming her as long as we need to, because she is toxic to other women, men and the society in general."* (USDF) Do Bad-fems think because women have a vagina, they are free of all moral obligations toward the society in which they live? Do they want men to keep up the same kind of behavior? Us, our group, with sensible women and men are appalled by this behavior. Freedom doesn't give anybody a blank check to do whatever they want. The sluts have responsibilities and moral obligations like everybody else. We mean that human beings are responsible for their genitals, even if the authority over that matter isn't always easy to reach.

It is a long chapter with a lot of mini paragraphs which are just introductions for ulterior development. We apologize for the brevity of some. The evolution and destruction of values isn't the point for us. We belong, as FDR said, to an old tradition of demolishing and rebuilding society. We were always able to keep some and bring new values which were the final justification of our revolutions. But for the first time some people play havoc with democracy, make it regress but are totally impotent to bring new values. Let's give our readers one more example of why we wrote our book.

We established quite clearly that Bad-fems are the ones

responsible for the destruction of the family unit. After half a century, let's look at the results of their claims. (bureau-Fatherless-children-in-america-statistics-120392, Liveabout.com)

- 13.6 million single parents are raising over 21 million children.
- 1 in 4 children live without a father.
- Suicide: 63% of youth consider suicide.
- Behavior disorder: 85% of all children exhibit behavioral disorder.
- High School dropout: 71% of juveniles in state-operated institutions.
- Substance abuse: 75% of adolescent patients in substance abuse centers.
- Aggression: 75% of rapists motivated by displaced anger.
- Runaways: 90% of runaway youths.
- Black children: 70% are born to a single mother.

CONCLUSION

The numbers above are catastrophic for millions and millions of children, mothers and fathers and the society in general. Contrary to what President Obama said: Men, millions and millions of them, didn't abandon their responsibility. It's worse, they forsook relationships with women thanks to a sexist, misandrist culture propagated by bad-fems. If women can't find any 'good men' well, let them know that men are in the same situation. They can't find any 'good women' when in fact we have plenty of both!

Too many men deal with women who think: "We don't need them. I have my job, my condo, my car; if they want me, they must jump through the hoops."

Well, what the Bad-fems didn't explain to them is that men don't jump, since they can buy a dinner for $10, wash their clothes for $5., own as well their condo, car, etc. Why do those young women under the influence of crappy-fems expect them to bother with a relationship based on suspicion or resentment? Both sexes are victims of that vicious kind of feminism. Women and men carry values used to constantly berate one sex and create a dramatic imbalance in the society. The social cost is horrendous, and it is going to get much worse before getting better for the reason that you have more and more men living alone, uncommitted, unmoored to any social duty and they have nothing to lose. Therefore, violence will rise since no human is around--just alcohol, pornography, drugs etc. It is already there; violence is utterly at random and affecting all social strata everywhere. People get punched in the face exiting the subway, stabbed leaving a beauty shop, shot in churches, schools, etc. by total strangers without any justification. Those acts are the expression of the deterioration of our social fabric. Are the Bad-fems responsible for everything wrong in society? No, they aren't, but they certainly share a huge responsibility with their political allies since there is a wide overpass between them, sexualists and radical racist minorities. It is the conjunction of the three of them which have such a negative impact on our society.

NOTES

1. What is Feminism, Sage Publication, London,1999
2. Brian D. Earp, 1 in 4 women: How the Latest Sexual Statistics were Turned into Click Bait by the "New York Times", huffpost.com, Sep. 28, 2016. Also see Christopher Krebs and Christine Lindquist, Setting the Record Straight on "1 in 5", Time.com/3633903/, December 15, 2004
3. Do we really have people who are using our Administration to advance their political opinions? We can't say but that case is certainly another example of the influence of Bad-fem politic in the Administration.
4. Who Stole Feminism, p. 11/12, Touchstone, 1994
5. Until proven innocent; Political Correctness and the Shameful Injustice of the Duke Lacrosse Rape Case', from K.C. Johnson and Stuart Taylor Jr., Thomas Dunne Books,) (see ADDENDUM)
6. Students must ask their professors for the sources which sustain their teaching. That way they will know that the origin of 'Whiteness' is from an in-depth interview of thirty white women based in Northern-California." Several being RadFems, Marxists, Lesbians, living in the same County as well as in San Francisco. Students must never forget the utter necessity of 'La raison de Esprit critique'.

SEXUALISTS

IN A PREVIOUS paragraph (**'women aren't unidimensional'**) we described the decline of numerous codes of behavior by RRM. One of the main casualties had been the idea of the 'moral superiority of women' which was a holdover from the more militant time of the Suffragettes and prohibition movements. Both of these movements used this idea to justify their political motives.

But after than half a century, nobody, women included, believes in the moral superiority, of women. Both sexes are equal.

Still, some women didn't seem particularly pleased with this specific aspect of equality. As a result, many attempted to imitate men in attitude and dress to fit in their new working world, as evidenced by the "power suit", that became a kind of uniform accepted by millions of women and popularized by many women in power, Hilary. Clinton among them.

yet, most importantly, the feminist, being aware of that loss of political "moral authority" power, try by any mean to get back some of that political power, to that end, the radicals took over the feminist movement and shepherd that resentment into "victimhood". This idea has resulted in many women seeing themselves as being victimized, mainly by men.

The consequences of Radfem concept of "Victimhood" has resulted in coercion of the society to satisfy, with means, including changing the laws, any claim from anybody who does not perceive herself as a victim. This is where Radfem political power rests and they use it, for example, to remove Due Process from the judicial system. Clearly, what we just wrote doesn't concern any woman being a <u>real</u> victims of gross injustices or crimes.

Nevertheless, 'Victimhood' became a cue, a green light, for many subgroups in our society to use for their own goals.

Sexualist is one of them.

Who are they? All people, groups, organizations who base their social identity on their sexuality. We have several organizations caring for the needs of homosexuals. One example is the LHBTQ, which evolved from a support group for equal treatment that we ourselves support, to a political party with which we disagree. "Heterosexual and homosexual into heavy duty pornography, pedophilia/child abusers, out of control S&M etc. any human being into any form of sexuality which is harmful to another human being is a sexualist." (USDF) But people into private libertinage aren't; the human body need some time to exult! Neither are any homosexuals who live their sexuality privately. The latest are barely noticeable and only the rabid homophobic looks for trouble with them. Our group thinks that personal sexuality must stay where it belongs, in the privacy of our lives and homes (which aren't a closet). When it became a public matter, for whatever reason, we all must live under some moral and social control; because sex is a time-bomb. It can be the most beautiful act (love) or destroy a human being (rape). Human sexuality isn't a toy for irresponsible people who for example make violence sexy in the media.

We shouldn't lose time running after the third banana of porno business but grab the attention of the ones who are making money from it. Pornographic violence, perversity, sadism is now everywhere on TV, cell phones, tablets, advertising, computers, video games, cables, movies, magazines, etc. and everybody is exposed to it. We should never forget that always some people, are paying some other people, to put pornographic violence on our screens. Those aren't ghosts floating incognito in an abstract system working on its own. It will be interesting to know who they are and ask them, politely first, to stop polluting our culture.

In this chapter, we are talking mainly about the group called the sexualists, whose basic theory is they are 'victims' of hetero-normativity, which doesn't recognize their need to satisfy their sexual freedom; meaning we must accept their sexuality, not as a personal choice, but as a social value. Consequently, the society must rewrite the definition of sexuality to make room for theirs. *"Sexuality - heterosexual or homosexual or any version of either - isn't a social value. It has never been."* (USDF) It belongs with food and water to the triptych of fundamental necessity, which supports all forms of life on this planet. We insist it has nothing to do with human values which are: Justice, Liberty, Love, Responsibility, Equality, Fraternity, Reliability, the deontology of the Ten Commandments, basically all principles which enhance and intensify the positive qualities of human beings, to make them better than they are.

One of the arguments that homosexuality cannot be a social value rests on the fact that there is no limit to sexual identities.[1] We can't define it. We have as many sexualities as we have humans on this planet. So, homosexuality can't be the 'new normal' since there is no normality in sexuality. All human society must be regulated. We must circumscribe it based first on its need, reproduction, and second the values of what is agreed upon by the population. These must be asserted. It is a human reality that, in the case of a democratic society, we must amalgamate, homogenize human sexuality in the general population as long as it doesn't put in jeopardy the basic function of it. Let's look further.

SEXUALITY, TRANSGENDERISM, HOMOSEXUALITY ETC.

Homosexuality isn't a pristine issue; it was tolerated by a lot of society if it was kept under control. It must be since the survival of any human society depends upon its reproduction capacity, and homosexuals don't reproduce themselves. With the assistance of others, some rich ones can have reproduction through surrogate women, frozen eggs and sperms etc. Still reproduction isn't on their agenda.

Alas, reproduction is a big issue for any human society. It's not a homosexual problem per se. For example, the Shakers, a small religious sect which didn't believe in human reproduction, disappeared slowly and peacefully in our society. They were a small number and didn't present any danger to our future. The Catharses comprise another similar group, but this time it was an important and powerful religious sect in southwest France which was exterminated by the authorities, the church, and much of the population because they were preaching that all nonreproductive sex was better than any reproductive sex. Half a million deaths later, the expression "Kill them all. God will know his own" originated from there. The population started to reproduce soon after. Nobody, for any reason whatsoever, religious, hedonistic, etc. can force a human society to be suicidal, because it is what's it's all about.

All human society knows that, depending of their environment, when they fall under a certain quota of population growth, they are under the constant threat of being invaded, men being killed, and women being enslaved (that's the basic), by the more populated, thus stronger society.

IT ISN'T THAT SPECIAL

So, homosexuality is an issue to look at very carefully.

How does the homosexual community see itself in our society? First, as we mentioned before, most of them are living their life generally in anonymity like the heterosexuals who don't especially talk about their sexuality. We are concerned here by the very active, dogmatic and politically intolerant homosexual leadership who, with their militants, try, and succeed, in changing laws of the country to fit their specific claims. Well, several decades ago laws to protect minority, including homosexual, were voted to fight any form of discrimination, lodging, employment etc. But it's not enough for the sexualists who always want more.

- First: We don't consider that being homosexual is so special. It is very dangerous to catalogue a group of people through their sexual preferences because it is similar to defining people by the color of their skin, religious affiliation, etc. They are creating one more ghetto in a society which already has too many of them, and they reinforce the de facto prejudice factors already existing in and out of those groups.
- Second: Wanting to be special, at any cost, can cause some to develop a militant link, for political advantages, to contrast their specificity with another minority such as the African American, and go as far as comparing their situation to the history of the slaves. They don't realize how offensive to black people is such a comparison. To assume that living as a homosexual in our society can be directly compared to the lives of Black people during Jim Crow in the South is absurd historically, and obscene humanly.
- Third: The homosexual community is right to fight for just treatment of their members. There is no reason on earth why some people are killed because of their sexuality. We can cite here the murder of a young homosexual man, Matthew Shepard, by a bunch of vicious murderers. But is it that unique? Four young men, on a spring break in Islip, Long Island, were so viciously murdered with machetes that their family couldn't

recognize them. They were simply at the wrong place at the wrong time. It happens all the time.

- Fourth: Jefferson Villalobos, Yensley Fuentes, Michel Banegas and Jorge Tigre were, we guess by their last name, from the Latino community. Are those young people not special because they aren't homosexual but heterosexual? Or are they special because they are from the Latino community? We should forget that nonsense of being special because of being homosexual. The atrocity of both cases doesn't call for any kind of differentiation.
- Fifth: But the sexualists are fond of being 'special' since we find now in the waiting room of hospitals leaflets reserved for homosexuals, and we suppose their "special" physical problems. So, we have two kinds of patients now, the 'special' ones who are homosexual, and the rest of us who aren't 'special'. It is not a good politic to push so hard to separate, to differentiate one from the rest of the general population. It's dangerous; they are opening the door to prejudice and racism against people who aren't 'special', who are going to react against the 'special' people who are perceived as racist.
- Sixth: If sexualists think they are 'special,' it implies that their needs are different from the rest of the population, and now we see everywhere in our society groups of people who are claiming they are 'special' for very different reasons: religious, ethnic, cultural, etc. They want to be different, and of course, everybody must overindulge on their specificity, otherwise you are an insensitive, racist, sexist pig, etc. Some Hasidim,

in Rockland County, NY, refuse vehemently to have their children vaccinated, exposing the rest of the population to measles. And, of course, for all these minorities, America is racist, religiously intolerant, a hell hole for them.

- Seventh: The rise of 'special' needs in our society, not only reinforces the sense of belonging to a small community, which always identifies itself against other communities, but also brings, when those minorities reach a critical mass, political claims based on the "specificity" of that group of people. Their political claims have nothing to do with the global welfare of the nation, nothing to do with the common good.

We should offer an idea of how it works for people who see themselves as 'special'. During the 2018 Winter Olympics, in Pyongyang Chang, a homo-skier did a good run and at the bottom of the hill all his friends were screaming, dancing etc. Absolutely nothing wrong with it, that skier certainly deserved encouragement from his friends. The only problem was they all were carrying the homo Rainbow flag, not one American flag was around. It is a sample of the consequences of the ghettoization of our society. That group of people doesn't feel, think, or understand, that they are American citizens first who happen to be homosexual and that really nobody cares about their sexual life.

Do we have to accept people's sexuality in our daily social discourse? Do we have to care what people are doing in the privacy of their bedroom? We belong to the people who made sure States got out of our bedroom! We didn't intend to let some people bring their bedroom into our social discourse 24/7/365! We are begging them to remain in the public discourse and, not forget, but keep their vagina, penis, anus, nipples, tongues, (you can put on that list any part of human body you like.) etc. in their bedroom where it belongs.

Megan Rapinoe, from the US soccer team, was pushed to some ridiculous extreme by the media. For sure, she is an exceptional athlete, has the right haircut, and a great smile, but we shouldn't forget, the World Cup was a team victory which routinely was occulted by her lesbianism. Nobody cares about her sexual preference; only the idiots who have nothing else to do, care. She is a great athlete, period. We don't care either that Serena Williams, also a great athlete, is heterosexual. But why does the media make Rapinoe's homosexuality a badge of honor to the extent that now you can base your social branding on it. You are a victim, you defeated the monstrosity of heterosexuality, you are a survivor, a hero etc. you are now a 'Star', because you are a lesbian. Does it have something to do with Ms. Rapinoe's political beliefs which is the LHBTQ+++, GLSEN etc. She is sponsored by eight major corporations, co-founder of a gender-neutral clothing line etc., in brief, someone rich, into social activism and politic. An interviewee offers us the following solution "She should take her lesbianism, put it in her gym bag and take it somewhere else than in the US Team, which represents us American people." All players of that team could be homosexual; it wouldn't change anything.

Sport has nothing to do with sex. If you bring it into sport, it will fuse with it and inevitably abuses will happen. So now there is no more team spirit but glorification, through sport, of the homosexuality of a 'star'. We had plenty of homosexual first-class athletes before. Most of them understood their talent had nothing to do with their sexuality since they were competing with many more heterosexuals able to reach the same level of sport greatness...

We don't want our girls to think that to be a recognized soccer star it sure helps to be homosexual. So now there is no more team spirit but glorification, through sport, of the homosexuality of a 'star'.

The case of Katie Sowers, assistant coach of the 49ers, is also interesting. Microsoft Corporation celebrated her lesbianism with several ads at $10.4 million *per minute*, during the Super Bowl. Microsoft is now a big supporter of lesbianism and replaces the tenacity, courage, cleverness, and experiences of that woman etc. by her sexual preferences? And naturally not a word about the team, the manager, the supporters, etc. The issue isn't with Katie Sowers but Microsoft.

We want our girls and boys to practice soccer or any sport available and be safe from abuses, especially sexual, because those can be devastating for life. All those cases of hetero or homosexual abuses happened in a general context of sex being free and easy. Well, it's not. Children victims of sexual abuses in schools, churches, sports activities, youth organizations etc. are the tragic witnesses of it.

But why are we drowning in sexualism in our culture? Well, let's look at the LHBTQ+++

THE LHBTQ+++'S IS NOW A FULL-BLOWN POLITICAL PARTY

Conversion therapy is a good start to understand why it is.

The homosexual lobby didn't like the Prayer therapy, so they call it Conversion therapy; but sexual or not, therapy never converts anybody. Everybody can use it as a tool to help resolve some mostly emotional and personal issues. There are numerous types of therapy: Music, Freudian, Jungian, writing, aroma, etc.

-   To insist on calling it a Conversion therapy are they afraid that the patient is going to be 'converted' to heterosexuality? And by doing so are losing the 'real religion' which is homosexuality? It's just ridiculous!
-   Homosexuals persist by saying that a "... Conversion therapy isn't a scientifically validated treatment and can, in fact, undermine self-esteem and be hazardous." (see Renee Binder, MD, governor.ny.gov). Since when are 'therapies' scientific? Psychotherapy, analysis, psychoanalysis, counseling as treatment, remedy, cure but certainly not scientific? Therapy is never scientific.
-   What is scientific is the research on brain function, the experimentation done with drugs, the fact-finding in biology, in genetics etc. but therapy is much closer to human healing; it is extremely difficult to do since humans are everything except 'scientific and rational'!

- Their next target can be any therapy which teaches thinking skills that people can use all their lives, or aromatherapy, or how about primal scream therapy? The radical homosexuals open the door for themselves to censure anything which doesn't fit their political program. We don't like it a bit, because they are giving themselves a right of censure on the American people.
- We don't accept it from the government; why should we accept it from them? The sexualist lobby, with the help of the media of course, can go as far as our living room. The show Will and Grace, in January 2018, shows how Will tried to save a youngster from being exposed to a 'prayer' therapy where his father sent him. That TV show was a perfect example of total homo propaganda in the media. It would be okay if the same TV channel was showing cases of successful prayer therapy, which can happen in a deeply religious family or group. But they never do.

We have doubt that prayer therapy will work on people like us who are basically, agnostic, atheistic or religiously Lite, in the sense of 'Bud lite'. The homosexuals' lobby is full of political posturing and contradiction because they want to implement homosexual support groups in our schools and are up in arms against prayer groups. We don't want either, since schools are a place where you learn about those issues.

We need to look at how manipulations of the public are done in that case.

How come the recall therapy, even more of a

controversial therapy, doesn't get the same approach? Is it because the sexualists, the Badfeminist etc., are using it to justify some of their allegations? They aren't concerned by social problems related to therapies but only by a certain kind of therapy; the one they judge has a negative impact on their influence. They use the executive action from Governor Cuomo the same way they use the Supreme Court to impose the homosexual marriage to advance their politic.

If some people think that a kind of therapy doesn't have any validity, and is useless, dangerous, and must be outlawed, it is their opinion. But why censuring it? Why don't we ask the opinion of the public before making it outlawed? Governor Cuomo used its action order (the President uses executive order) to announce all multi-agency regulations that "today ban public and private health care insurers from covering the practice in the State and also prohibit various mental health facilities from conducting the practice on minors" to get prayer therapy. Where did he get the right to interfere when people are using a private insurer? Further we can read on his website "conversion therapy – which refers to therapy intended to change an individual's sexual or gender identity – has been repudiated by many...", but, here again, we did some research and who are the many people? So far, the ones we found were homosexual themselves or those very close to their lobby. Governor Cuomo should be the first one to insist on making as many issues possible part of a public debate. That's the democratic way to do politics.

His pandering to the homosexual lobby cannot be done to the detriment of the democratic process. But how far can the sexualists go? Well, people, straight to our kindergartners! In page 70 we give example of drag queens in full regalia being invited to kindergartens, bookstores, public libraries etc. to give lectures to children.

The LHBTQ+++ obtrude now in the selection of which actor can play a role or not. They pushed away a heterosexual actress from playing a transgender because she isn't one. Actors must fight that preposterous intrusion of the sexualists/LHBTQ+++ into their profession; because sooner or later they won't be able to play, like Jim Parsons, an autistic heterosexual since he isn't one. They must defend and keep their freedom to play any characters they want. You don't need to be hetero to play such a character, see Rock Hudson be a handsome hetero hunk in his movies, when homo in his private life, neither to be a French man when on screen, see Kevin Kline in French kiss. French people thought he was more french than a french!

FROM GAY MARRIAGE TO POLYGAMY

We were among the people from the left who said that the gay marriage was a Pandora's box, that uncoupling marriage from procreation would have huge social consequences. We were called homophobic, racist pigs, bigots etc. that prejudice, intolerance, fear, etc. were the causes of our reaction. We had a lot of arguments but let us make it simple; we were right, and they were wrong, because now, we have groups of people who want to go to the next step, which is polygamy, but masquerades as 'plural marriage' or even better, the cunning 'polyamourous'. They aren't making too much effort to bring new arguments; they are the same as for the homosexual marriage.

"There is no longer a strategic reason to hold off," and the cynicism of Fredrik DeBoer is quite explicit in the following quote: "To advocate for polygamy during the marriage equality fight may have seemed to confirm the socially conservative narrative, that gay marriage augured a wholesale collapse in traditional values...".[2] Naturally, polygamy 'is a human right' and we are surprised that Mr. DeBoer didn't yet bring the argument of the 'civil rights issue'. The fact remains that, like homosexuality, polygamy isn't a 'human right" because its rationalization is the same as for the homosexual marriage. Conor Friedersdorf wrote a very useful article on that subject.[3] For our group, being against homosexual marriage wasn't based on socially conservative arguments, but because we knew some alternative already existed in North America and Europe that the narrow-minded, dogmatic, illiberal homosexual leadership refused to adapt to our situation.

From Canada's Quebec State originates the idea that people for very different reasons should be able to associate themselves under the protection of the law. That idea migrated to Germany which improved it. France, noticing that innovation, took it and extended it to the point that now 50% of their people live in common under the "Pacte civil de Solidarite" (Civil Pact of Solidarity). Brother and sister can manage a family farm when parents are too old. Two roommates with limited income can buy an apartment, two people of the same sex who aspire to share their lives can live together, etc. These are protected under that new type of judicial structure.

The homosexual lobby chooses instead a disingenuous way by going to the Supreme Court and having the 'gay marriage' crammed down everybody's throat, thanks to one vote majority in the Supreme Court. They just don't trust American Democracy, and it means also that a minority can now impose its will on the majority. It is incompatible with the tenets of what democracy is. The homosexuals lobby opened the door to any small interest group who wants to dominate our nation. Are we so retrograde, stupid, and unsophisticated that our citizenry can't express its opinion wisely through a State referendum? Through a nation-wide referendum? Well, it is certainly the opinion of sexualists. We are really concerned by the constant weakening of all democratic institutions by groups which want to alter our way of living. There is no valid reason why a small group of people can by-pass the democratic process and impose its will on the general population.

It is not the responsibility of the Supreme Court to make decision on how we want to live. It is the Congress and the Senate which must promulgate the Laws which must express the Values and the Will of the people who elected them.

THE CONSEQUENCES OF POLYGAMY

How is polygamy working in the real world? During the last six years, hundreds of teenage boys have been expelled or felt compelled to leave the polygamous settlement that straddles Colorado City, Ariz., and Hilldale, Utah. Disobedience is usually the reason given for expulsion, but former sect members and state legal officials say the exodus of males (the expulsion of girls is rarer)—also remedies a huge imbalance in the marriage market. Members of the sect (s) believe that to reach eternal salvation, men are supposed to have at least three wives.

If we look at a world map, we see where polygamy is settled. It is basically where the Muslim religion is implanted, so the roots of polygamy are mainly in Islam. As far as we know, the US has only a tiny fraction in the Muslim and Christian communities practicing polygamy. Why should we change our way of living for them? What is the logic behind such a claim? The polygamists are lucky to reside in a country where they can live the way they want, thanks to the separation of Church and State. Secularism gives them the freedom necessary to practice their religion. But what makes them think our society has the obligation to deal with the consequences of their religious beliefs? To take care of all those young men expelled from the polygamist sect, because they're a burden to the older male.

Freddie de Boers didn't let his readers know which countries abandoned, renounced polygamy. Well, Japan did it in 1880, China in 1953, India 1955, Nepal 1936, etc. even if polygamy still exists in some parts of India the government pushes hard to eliminate it. There is certainly some good reason why those countries choose monogamy![4]

We can write that the emergence of institutional monogamy in Europe was one of the main factors which helped first, tribes, cities, and societies to progress the way they did. Because a family unit composed of a man, a woman and a few children, oblige them to focus on their family unit as a way to increase their welfare. Increasing the labor force was primordial. Now in our modern society sending our children to college, buying houses, etc. are very powerful factors of social stabilization, while polygamy has exactly the opposite effect due to the scattering of attention on too many children.

THE DELIGHT OF SEXUAL FREEDOM

Every human should be free to express its sexuality, is the motto of the sexualists. We certainly agree, as long it is in the limit and within the tenets of respected and agreed upon, social values. No way is their statement true: you just want to crush our sexuality with your heteronormativity. No, we don't, but we can't let the wife of a well-known lesbian entertainer, at 14 years of age justified for "being in a rampage against (her) classmates in high school"! This is why we don't want any of the Asia Argentos, Epsteins, etc., who can't control their desires and urges, to do more damage around us, under the cover of their sexual freedom, since we, homosexuals and heterosexuals, are the ones paying the consequences of it.

The sexualists, as well as numerous media, entertainment corporations, etc. are responsible for the obscene sexualization of our social life. *"We have no obligation to let OUR society be under the constant pressure and influences of their obsessive carnality. Neither do we have to let any corporations exploit, and make profit, by using continually the most primitive fundamental constitutive social oscillation, (sexual pulsation), inherent to any human society. Humans and their sexuality aren't a byproduct, an outcome of economic activities."* (USDF) We can think whatever we want about human, that they are "The measure of all things" (Protagoras) or "A reasoning animal" (Seneca) or even "Nature's sole mistake" (W.S. Gilbert) it doesn't matter, but we all know that they aren't what a magazine editor, a marketing department etc. want them to be.

WHY ARE WE CONCERNED BY THE AFTERMATH OF SEXUALISTS' POLITIC?

Pornography awards on Chanel #386 -TMC W –include BEST IN SEX, 2015 AVN: Best New Starlet: Carter Cruse, Best Actor: Steven St. Croix, Best Anal Sex: Adriana Chechik and Manuel Ferrara, etc. Why such an award? As one of the female presentations said: "Anal sex is the Lamborghini of sex." It was on a cable show at 3:00 AM. Do we have a problem with it? Not really, because as one of our couple interviewees said "those adult people can park a truck in their ass h…, we can't care less, as long as they stick to their little Porno-World. They are adults and it is their responsibility." In a word they must remain discreet and go underground, it is the best place where they can do their stuff, which exists for millennia! Any state can let them exist at a low level and keep them under control with judicious laws.

This is not where the real problem is for us.

In 2016/2017, we have an example which should have never happened. It will illustrate quite well why we are so concerned about the out of control sexualism of Badfem and sexualists.

Vogue Teen Magazine, which had a target marketing from 11 to 17 years old, promoted anal sex. Let's begin with the head of that publication, Mrs. Vintour, the Queen of Fashion, Artistic Director of Condé Nast, hired E. Welteroth, who, as an Editor in Chief, published a piece called Anal sex: what you need to know. How to do it right.

Mr. Phillip Picardi, digital editorial director, published what is a promotion of anal sex to underage people. The author of the article is, Gigi Engel, a New York City sex educator.

What the hell is a sex educator, named Gigi Engel, who promotes and teaches, not only anal sex, but all kind of sexual activities, masochism, sadism etc., it's how she is making a living. What is she doing writing such an article in a teen magazine?

Who is E. Welteroth to advocate that kind of practice to all young people from minorities that she is so fond of? The indecency of that woman is kind of epic!

Who is P. Picardi and who helped her to publish such a heavy-handed, oafish, stupid and insensitive article? His homosexuality isn't an excuse for his boorishness. He isn't a "victim" of homophobia, as he pretends, but of his own vulgarity and lewdness.

Who were the people responsible at Condé Nast for allowing such a publication?

Why didn't Mr. Bob Sauerberg stop the publication of that article?

Which initiative the Newhouse publishing Company, (legal name: Advance Publications), under the management of Mr. Steven, Jonathan, Donald Newhouse and Mr. Thomas Summer, CFO, took regarding that scandal, and we repeat, which should have never happened! They are at the head of a $12 billion conglomerate. They can't overview everything going on in their business, but they have the responsibility to choose people who do their job properly by implementing decency and responsibility in their company. Instead, what we saw is the expression of a sexualist culture completely debased from social responsibility and values and this is now penetrating every level of our culture.

We can't acquiesce silently to pornography and homo-sexuality as a standard of sexual activity because the consequences of it are catastrophic for people, especially the youngest. Now we have a ten-year-old girl with throat cancer (HPV) because she is habituated to fellatio; we have a 12-year-old boy who practices strangulation as an erotic act on 'girlfriend' since he saw it in porn and thought it would give her an orgasm, etc. Social responsibility is something important, certainly as much as our sexual freedom.

(We made an exception in listing the names of the people involved in that story, because we are dealing with the consequences of that kind of sexual politic every day. Let's look now at that problem but at another angle.)

In Massachusetts, the school system, in 2013/2014 was distributing a book on sexual education to children starting at ten years old. It was so graphic and shocking that the Washington Post and the NYT rejected the ads. Well, if it is too graphic for those publications, we understand very well why Mrs. Contrada found appalling the callousness of people responsible for exposing young people to that kind of pornography under the cover of sexual education, *that we are in favor of.* [5] Us, We, our group, FROM THE LEFT, support her fight against pornography in schools. We prefer to work on some issues, with anybody Christian, atheist, people of any color, conservative women and men, than to hang out with people from the sexualist crowd. We won't hesitate to work with Bernie Sanders' people on some issues than to keep being manipulated by pretenders of liberalism who are just whited sepulchers! To sum up, our position on that issue "We would unite with anybody to do right and with nobody to do wrong" (Frederick Douglass).

Sex can be fun, interesting, tempting, riveting, etc. and we all are big fans of it. It gives a lot of pleasure and creating life is the cherry on top of it. We can read about it, look at fabulous paintings showing it, see interesting, captivating movies about it, even 'walk on the wild side of it' and we intend to keep being involved in it. At the same time, we respect the boundaries necessary to make us live together. We applaud that mother who called the police on a heterosexual couple having intercourse on the beach in the middle of the afternoon! (she was next to them with her children.) [6]

The insistence of the sexualists to enforce their sexual politic on the general population is a grave miscalculation. To fight sexual discrimination, prejudice etc. is absolutely justified, as well as educating people on the reality of homosexuality. We made some substantial progress. But it is impossible to satisfy the claims of people like the one following the LHBTQ+++, since there is no limit_to it. Sex is the cornerstone of their politic period!

But our newspapers explain to us that the heterosexuals would be much happier "...if they took a few lessons from their same-sex counterparts." Naturally, in the 'lessons' heterosexuals must learn is to share dishwashing which is "...the core that most influences relationship quality." What kind of idiotic argument is that? Is it a farce? Around 70% of households own a dishwasher! Women and men don't wash dishes; they load machines which do the job for them. When we write about the decay of our intellectual life, this is what we are talking about because we found that quote in the NYT. [7]

That free propaganda for homosexuality isn't innocuous. It is a spin to introduce homosexuality as equal to heterosexuality.

Well, we insist, it is not equivalent, it is not consistent with the development of any Society. Binary sexuality is multiform since it's practiced by humans who have as much imagination as their homosexual counterpart but somehow, they know their sexuality has a sense of purpose.

People into nonbinary sexuality are inflamed by it and think the existence of binary sexuality is a constant threat to their sexuality that they put forward as the ultimate expression of freedom. Well, it isn't; because under the cover of the sexual freedom, they give themselves more and more rights over our way of living, to the point of prescribing Puberty Blockers to children from 10 years old and up. It eunuchizes boys and girls to go straight to menopause. We develop at length the consequences of it in our chapter infosphere/media. So, we want them to know that binary sexuality is here to stay.

The sexualists, as well as some people from entertainment, Badfem, media, corrupt business, all have full responsibility for the explosion of random sexual violence, venereal diseases, and more that we are witnessing every day everywhere. Twenty years ago, we saw our 10-year-old daughters dancing in front of a mirror, singing, "One more time, baby" that their MTV idol, 16-year-old Britney Spears, was singing and dancing in the hallway of a mid-school, wearing a kiddy porn outfit. MTV, the Badfem, the sexualists were never infuriated by the exploitation of children's unformed sexuality. They wanted to free very young girls from "patriarchal domination"! They never saw the pedophiles/child abusers of "free the children" waiting in the dark alleys of human sexuality. After thirty years of porno hard core to porno smut, we must deal with the results of it. Pornography, which includes sexualism, is all over our schools, churches, youth associations, sport activities etc. [8]

TRANSGENDERISM CAN HELP TO UNDERSTAND HUMAN SEXUALITY

Human sexuality is a difficult subject that we must handle with care. We have some cases of women who feel they are men and vice-versa. There is no reason for us not to believe them. They go through hormone therapy, spend a lot of money on medical procedures and think and live like the opposite sex. Some have the beards and guts to fit in the society as men. Still at some point some want to have a child. Their genital apparatus being female, they can give birth to a child and happily for she/him, if they didn't have a mastectomy, are even able to breast feed their babies and they do. So, for us the radical sexualists' definition of homosexuality doesn't reflect the reality of what homosexuality is. It is a much more complex issue that we must simplify, than 'if you feel homosexual, you are homosexual.' The example we have just given is in total opposition to that claim. David Bowie, who had wide knowledge of human sexuality, once said: "You have no idea how many straight men are in the gay closets." We can apply the same quote to lesbians who have no idea how many heterosexual women are in their closets.

We have an undeniable genetic identity, which can't be superseded. We can't vacate nature-based reality just to please ourselves. But we humans are a bunch of developed, multifaceted, labyrinthine... So, things are much more complicated for us due to the way we live in an environment created by us called civilizations. Each of those carry their own cultural definition of sexuality. *"The insistence of some homosexuals on changing the definition of human sexuality ad infinitum, to satisfy any of their desires, is just homo delirium"*. (USDF)

Nonetheless, the ones we want to protect first are kids, with 'tendency' or 'confusion" or 'incertitude' about their sexuality. A very small minority of them will be homosexual, still all must have access to any kind of therapy, counseling, guidance available. It can relieve their anxiety, pain, distress inasmuch as their insecurity. The massive rush of hormones doesn't make anybody homosexual or transgender. It's a difficult transitional period in everybody's life. Some people are preying on their tender age and incertitude to satisfy their sexual perversion. It is those people we should watch out for, and we find them among homosexuals and heterosexuals.

We don't know exactly why some babies are born homosexual! We have scientific evidences which point toward "Gene", which is stable, but "Epigenome" is instable. Melissa Healey wrote an article in the latimes.com regarding the research done in the field of genetics, it's interesting and opens a door which can explain why in some families everybody is straight and one child is homosexual [9]. If the explanation of homosexuality can be decoded at the molecular level, being homophobic is an aberration; as well as being heterophobe, since we don't control our genetic mark-up. To deny it is an absurdity frequently endorsed by the radical homosexual militants.

Let's look now at how far the Sexualists can go.

In Paris, the sculptor, Paul McCarthy, put Place Vendome, one of the most select addresses of the French Capital, a fifty foot "anal plug" (butt plug) as a Christmas tree. You could buy a replicate in chocolate as souvenir. So, a grandfather and his granddaughter had the following dialogue. 'Pappy, what is that big green thing?' – It's a butt plug disguised as a Christmas tree, sweetie. – What is a butt plug, grandpa? – It's something grown-ups put in their ass h.... to feel it's Christmas every day. – Pappy, can I have a chocolate one? Etc.'

The homosexual lobby is pushing the envelope very hard everywhere. A homo couple insisted on having their wedding cake made by the only bakery who didn't want to do it, when four others, in the same town, were ready to take their order. That form of dogmatic militant activism is a direct call for trouble, since that logic makes it acceptable to wear a jacket with 'homosexuality is a sin', 'homosexuality sucks!', 'being homosexual is unhealthy' etc. in a gay bar. Both ways to proceed will bring more intolerance for the offending side, more social violence and our social life will suffer because of it. Let's have another sample.

We have now some 'drag queens' in full regalia, who are reading stories to our children in schools, bookstores, libraries. Did anybody responsible for those events speak to educators, psychologists, parents, teachers about the impact on very young children, from 3 to 12 years, how they assimilate, comprehend those strange and scary personages? How they fit into their imagination? A 'drag queen' isn't a funny clown. It's not a fictitious creature. It's a human being, an entertainer, who, depending on the role, bring parody, sex, lampoon, travesty, farce, pasquinade etc. We enjoy their talent because they entertain us the adults.

But be in kindergartens? Children walk around holding a precious little furry thing to reassure them, and we have now some fucked up people who bring in full regalia, people who are caricatures of the adults who are supposed to protect them. Children don't need to be exposed to incomprehensible and traumatic personages who don't belong to their world. They need Big Bird, Ernie and Bert, Sponge Bob. The sexualists' rationale is that we must expose children to reality early to fight prejudice. So, why don't we introduce them to homosexuality, drugs, horror movies, guns ... After all, it belongs to our social life. Children's world is already full of anxiety, so we must be very careful when invading their space. (NYPL online, Drag Queen Story Hour, by Yuhua Hamasaki, for grade-k-2, May 1st, 2020.)

In conclusion, if we liken the sexualists' treacherous game to that of Eros and Thanatos, we see its forbidding end - because in that game Thanatos is always the victor. Alas, it is only by creating life that we are able to defeat death.

Another comparison might be made between the sexualists and the myth of Icarus, trying in vain to reach the sun. The sexualists seem to believe that they will arrive at ultimate freedom by satisfying their primitive pulsion from the deep dark fringe of Mother nature. We are, all of us still so close to it, but civilization mercifully, is based upon the subjugation of human basic instincts, otherwise we will be devouring each other.

NOTES

1. See Wikipedia's LGBTIQCAPGNGFNBA+++ etc.
2. It's Time to Legalize Polygamy, politico.com, June 26, 2015.
3. The Case Against Encouraging Polygamy, theatlantic.com, July 9, 2015
4. Media contact for UCB, basil.waugh@ubc.ca)
5. See her testimony: Porn in Massachusetts schools – joint Committee on the judiciary – May 7, 2013, "I am speaking in support of House Bills 1282 and 1477" is where you can find her Speech
6. see Ruby Warrington, inside Teen Vogue: our readers consider themselves activists", the guardian.com, Sat 25 Feb. 2017; and, Peter Barbara, Teen vogue Editor Flips off Critics of Anal Sex article, blames backlash on homophobia", LifeSiteNews.com, Wed. Jul. 19, 2017
7. see Review Section, Sunday, February 16, 2020
8. ("STDs rates rise drastically in 2015" (Teen Vogue), "STDs on the rise" (www.cdc.gov), "Why so Many American Teens Have STDs" (time Magazine). The study made by the CDC about STD (Sexual Transmitted diseases) is a good source of information.)
9. Scientists find DNA differences between gay men and their straight twin brothers, (see latimes.com, Oct. 8, 2015. Article based on UCLA Molecular biologist Tuck C. Nugget researches

RADICAL MINORITIES (RRM)

"Ignorance, the root and stem of all evil." Plato

"But for the National welfare, it is urgent to realize that the minorities do think and think about something other than the race problem." Zora Neale Hurston

"If we are so cruel to minorities, why do they keep coming here?" Ann Coulter

"If you don't like something, change it. If you can't change it, change your attitude." Maya Angelou

"Let's us not seek to satisfy our thirst for Freedom by drinking from the cup of bitterness and hatred." Martin Luther King

IMMIGRATION:

Let's start with immigration, because immigrants are the minorities of tomorrow. We are, from the beginning, a country founded on immigration. There are three kinds of immigration: legal, illegal and refugees.

Legal immigration has been well under control since the Naturalization Act of 1798, just eleven years since the signing of the Constitution. It has never been an unregulated invasion of our country. In 1868 the 14th Amendment protected children by offering them citizenship at birth, in 1870 Black people became citizens, in 1882 the Chinese Exclusion Act kept those people out of the US. At one point or another the sick, mentally unstable, Communist, uneducated, and homosexuals were barred from entering the US. During the Great Depression, President Hoover closed the borders to all kinds of immigration and pushed for voluntary or forced repatriation. Between 1.5 to 2.5 million were sent back to Mexico and Europe. In 1952 the McCarran-Walter Immigration and Naturalization Act upheld our long-held immigration quota system but does not mention ethnicity. The Immigration Reform and Control Act which involved 3 million illegal immigrants even though it had limited access to millions. With that quick summary we can see that immigration is a constant in our national politics.

Our party, during the '60s, really thought that America could resolve the world's problems. We were wrong. Instead, the problems of the world came to America. We used to have a stable immigration policy with a quota of 70% reserved for Irish, English, and German and the rest open to other countries, (CIS.org). The Hart-Cellar Act opened the gate to a massive immigration, the largest ever in our country: over 19 million, triple the number of what was admitted in the previous

30 years, came to our shores. We aren't including illegal immigration. Some estimation puts that total number at around 33 million people. But our Party shifted from managing immigration to care for the immigration rights over the rights of the general population. The ones affected the most by it are the first- and second-generation immigrants who paid their dues to be American citizens and see their status and situation constantly threatened by waves of new immigrants.

"The people of Ethiopia have the same right to come to the United States under this bill as the people from England, the people of France, the people of Germany, [and] the people of Holland," griped Senator Sam Ervin, a conservative Democrat from North Carolina. "With all due respect to Ethiopia, I don't know of any contributions that Ethiopia has made to the making of America.[1]

We have another category of people entering our country called refugees. It is another category by itself. We won't discuss that matter in this book.

ILLEGAL IMMIGRATION:

Around 12 to 15 million people is a serious issue. Many come from Mexico; they are the poorest of the poor. They were ruined by NAFTA which had a positive impact on the industrialization in Mexico and the rise of a middle class but caused serious problems for poor farmers. So many lost their land and then had a choice between working for drug cartels or moving to America. The greater number moved to the U.S., putting unprecedented pressure on the existing legal Latino community, which now had to face competition for immigrants ready to work for lower paying jobs. It explains why so many Hispanics from Texas to California, voted for Donald Trump, as incomprehensible as that was to Democrats. They didn't understand that their unconditional support for unfettered immigration was stabbing the American Latino and Black community in the back. Our Party misunderstood so much about the consequences of our lack of immigration policy.

Lyndon Johnson, in justifying new immigration legislation, said, "It does not affect the lives of millions. It will not restructure the shape of our daily lives." Robert Kennedy added "It will increase the amount of authorized immigration by only a fraction." Senator Claiborne Pell insisted that "contrary to the opinions of some of the misinformed, this legislation does not open the floodgates." Our leadership did not anticipate the consequences of opening the gates without any coherent immigration policy, and they still don't in 2020! These immigrants are now in the worst position, exploited mercilessly, unemployed, and from an unstable underground where there is no hope. It's kind of rotten situation for them, since de-industrializations of our country removed most low-level jobs used by immigrants as a step stool for their integration in the US.

MINORITIES:

Disclosure: We aren't color blind and feel sorry for people who are.

For Badfem, women are victims of men, sexualists are victims of heterosexuals, and RRM are victims of white people. That's too many who think they are victims!

Some of our group belong to minority groups. It is clear to us that the large multitude of minorities are people who get up in the morning, go to work, worry about their children, and pay their bills. When the media says that racism is the full-time job of the American people, it's total lunacy.

Does racism exist? Of course, it does. The destruction of Korean-owned businesses by Black rioters in Los Angeles in 1992 was certainly as racist an act as there is. During the LA riots, 45% of all property damaged was Korean-owned businesses. It was what the Korean people call the Sa-I-Gu, a racist attack on American citizens from the Korean community. Does it mean that all black people are rabid racists? Certainly not. All social groups have in their ranks a certain percentage of hardcore racists. So, we want to focus on those radical racist groups and see what they are up to.

"Individual rights are not subject to a public vote; a majority has no right to vote away the rights of a minority; the political function of rights is precisely to protect minorities from oppression from majority."

The above are words written by Ayn Rand, the mother goddess of the free-market conservative movement and a hero to many with libertarian agendas; the darling of pure capitalism if you wish. Isn't it incongruous to see radical minorities sharing a similar ideology with a group of elitist white people who are themselves a mini minority? What is wrong with our radical minorities? Do they want to try on the shoes of the SuperConglos. We should let them know right away that those shoes are too big for their feet. [2]

But a nation can't be governed by minorities, especially, micro-minorities which have a limited understanding of government for all and by all. Their political programs are defined by their interests only.

THIS IS WHY WE HAVE A CONSTITUTION

A nation is built by people having a land, the USA, a language, English, and a culture in common emerging from a combination of subcultures. Most nations, have a "principal," which is a massive block of humanity, who based their co-habitation on a certain number of transcendental values which supersede their social differences, color of skin, their religious or political beliefs etc. All the differences and contradictions inherent to our nation are unified under our Constitution.

The power emerging from that Constitution is awesome since it is the sum of all citizens' will.

That power is divided into three co-equal branches of government, Judicial, Executive and Legislative.

The system works smoothly because it is based on a minimum set of values shared by all people, which transcends all individual interests.

Norms are the applications of the values and it is what we are dealing with every day in our lives.

"The 'Bill of Rights' is, and was always, the moderator of the Constitution, never a substitute for it." (USDF)

That is basically how a democratic government works. We must remember, that it is that Constitution, unique in the World, which obliges all the parochial, illiberal, dogmatic, racist people, from all religions, colors, ethnicities who came from everywhere and live freely here to tolerate and accept each other, thanks to the protection of the laws. It created, by the same token, a nation. Our country never, ever had any cultural, national or ethnic homogeneity. What can an orthodox Jew from Brooklyn and a homosexual militant from Los Angeles, a Swedish farmer from North Dakota and a singer from New Orleans have in common? Not that much. What makes them live together is the Constitution, shored up by a democratic government.

It certainly took time to make all of us live under such an umbrella and create a real nation. But why are we obliged, in 2020, to remind the public of such basic facts? Well, our RRM are adamant against our Constitution, since the latest isn't based on their specific minorities but on the aggregate collection of people now from all over the world. We will see later how the RRM intend to weaken it to such an extent that they could dismantle – (deconstruct will be their word of choice) - our country. Do they think it will be done peacefully? Do they understand that without that Constitution we will be killing each other? All this because they don't want to recognize that a majority, itself an assemblage of minorities, has the right to live according to their agreement on values and thus be in charge. Let's see what our RRM have in mind.

WHITENESS PART I

We quote Michael E. Dyson below because his words are representative of the work of some other prominent African Americans and mirror the opinion of the RRM.

"If you are white, this Country is a safe giant space."

"Success is easier for white people due to systemic privilege."

"White people should be taxed due to their white privilege." [3]

"Whites should open Individual Reparation Accounts... for young black people".

Another quote can illustrate this matter of contention.

"The white Identity that's been rendered invisible and neutral because it's seen as objective and universal...." (meaning, is it like Noble Gasses?) We don't pay attention to how whiteness is one among racial identity...that's what people of color do when they challenged whites' privilege and unconscious bias."

That is the basic of the whiteness theory.

Did the authors of it comprehend that they resurrected the *concept of blackness that we try since the end of the Civil War to get rid of?* If you use color and race to resolve a social problem you are reintroducing race, implicating racialism, bigotery, anti-semitism etc. and it has a catastrophic impact. For example, Police shooting of black people is 32% and white is 54% of all casualties. But black people are 13% of the population when white are around 75%. We certainly have a discrepancy, but blackness concept makes you able to ignore 60% of white and 14% of Latino / Asians, since only 'Black Lives Matters'. This is why we favor 'All Lives Matter" (ALM)

Let's bring a few people into the conversation.

This is what Chimamanda Ngozi Adichie [4] said during an interview, "In Nigeria, I wasn't black. I didn't think of myself as black. When I go back home now, when I got back to Nigeria now, I get off the plane in Lagos and

I just don't think of race." And she adds "So if somebody is an Ass H..., and many people are, I think they have a bad day. They are Ass H.... They don't like her. Right. If it happens in the US, all those things, and I'm thinking also they are racist." Let's hope that Mr. Dyson read what a successful black female writer noticed about her blackness and racial identity.

"Racism is a reality, but it also can be a construed idea, a political concept used for whatever you need it for." (USDF) Opportunists apply it when, for example, Mr. Dyson and friends, are confronting certain types of situations.

Spike Lee also can shed some light to how minorities see the race issue. He called slavery: "a Holocaust." [5] This spoken during an interview explaining that it was the argument used to keep Norman Jewison from directing the Malcolm X movie, because he lacked "the deep understanding of the black psyche."

There was never any holocaust against Black people as a group for the simple reason that they had a monetary value, and if Mr. Spike Lee knows the psyche of the white, some are certainly able to treat people like shit but never take it as far as killing them *if they have any monetary value!* This is not because they had any love or respect for them, but because they would have to buy another slave, and it costs money. For example, they whipped runaway slaves, they didn't kill them. We certainly had murders of slaves by their owners, as well as rape and atrocious flogging. But it wasn't like the tragedy of the Holocaust, which was since Jews as human, didn't have any 'Value', including monetary. If they had any, the Nazis would have sold them!

And Mr. Ta Nehisi Coates, a writer of novels, thinks

that slavery created America; we can say that it existed before since the port to receive their load of slaves and goods were in place. The headright system and the baselines already shaped plantations; all structures were ready to receive their human cargo since there weren't enough people to work on the lands stolen from the Indians. In 1524, Antoine De Conflans discovered the Bay of New York. Black people were living in America before slavery started, as indentured servants or free men as well as white people. [7]

These declarations about slavery creating America distort the real history of it. It doesn't need any baseless affirmations to help communicate its many horrors. However, by adding some "new facts" every other day, the fires of racism are stoked for racist political opportunism. The only difference is now, thanks to Enlightenment's rationality we now know in detail why and how it happened. That understanding gives us better tools to fight it, but it doesn't mean we will always be successful.

Mr. Ta Nehisi Coates' loudly proclame that slavery created not only America but Capitalism.

History is a very serious discipline since it is the memory bank of human society. Any opinion not sustained with significantly verifiable fact (s), is an 'intellectual fart', aka logical fallacy. Nobody owns the 'Facts', nobody can change them. Too many people think it is their God-given right to do it and Mr. Ta Nehisi Coates is one of them. In future publications we will remind him some basic facts about the history of industry and cotton which started in England-India-Egypt and not in America.

A WHITE KNEE ON A BLACK NECK (GEORGE FLOYD)

We are revolted when seeing someone asphyxiated by a cop pressuring his knee on a black neck. He has a completely empty look in his eye, like he was somewhere else. To see that video certainly justifies all the emotional reactions. Of course, following it, we have had our usual riots with destruction of properties, looting, a few deaths here and there. Why are we so casual about the violence? Well, it's been like that for the last 70 years, hasn't it? If we still have some people on the street it is due to Corvi-19 and its millions of unemployed people. Will we be able to resolve something this time?

We hope, but don't think so.

To change for the better our way of policing our Society, we must revamp our way of thinking and living. Are we ready to put some basic values back in place? Are we prepared to fight all the businesses which are polluting our culture with obscene violence? Are we inclined to take on our obscene consumption of drugs? Are we up for running after the one who is corrupting our Democracy with their money? Are we geared up to face the consequences of 'defunding the police'? Can we put together a political coalition which will bring some real progress right now? The answer is no to each of those questions. Police violence is just the tip of the iceberg.

Let's start with the reason number one. Our social life has been emptied of its values, so we don't have anything around to unify us. People's fighting is based only on the subjectivity of their feelings. As honorable as those might be it won't give them the political steadfastness, the might necessary to change anything fundamental in the society.

As one of the interviewees said, "To make it simple, our system is 'f......g broken'! We must restore it." And we add, first, we must send back all the radical groups to where they belong, the fringe of our society. They are a permanent obstacle to any form of dialogue between us, which is necessary to build a 'coalition of the willing' to replace that dreadful 'coalition of the incompetent'.

We can't count on any radicals to explain the following. A study shows police at sky-high risk *for suicide compared to almost any profession.* That is a form of violence we must talk about, since it is a statement regarding what the police must deal with (Jena Hillard, addictioncenter.com, Sept. 14,2019) meaning our police force reflects what we are. Some of them are violent because some of us are violent, and violence is a consequence not a cause.

In our book we give a few arguments other than racism which is used now as the ultimate explanation for everything wrong in America. So, to reinstitute racism and 'slavery' as a permanent social fact is a good trick to avoid all other annoying issues we mention above.

We don't ask anybody to share our opinions. We don't want to convince anybody of anything. We welcome and need the *exchange* of ideas, arguments etc. The first step is to never accept any preposterous affirmations just to advance a political agenda. Do we have racists, thieves, misogynists, murderers, imbeciles etc. in our country? Yes, we do, unfortunately, just as in every other nation on this planet! But what's authentically convincing for our people with that revisionist's history of the South and slavery? NYT '1619'? Walter Johnson's, *The Broken Heart of America*, makes St. Louis a hot bed of imperialism and racism, which was the same as everywhere else at the time. Its historically nonsense based on a misconceived understanding of what imperialism is.

The question for us is why are we saturated by a propaganda about American people being racist, like we are living in the deep South in 1900? Does it have something to do with the coming election? Is it a contrivance built to replace our nonexistent political program? Let us look further, because we are afraid it is.

ABOUT PEOPLE WHO MOVED HERE.

When we write about past events, we have the intellectual obligation to respect the frame of historical references of that past. Who were the people who emigrated here, what was their background? Landing in Cape Cod or Jamestown didn't give them a brand-new brain or memory. They came from countries where they were slaughtering each other, where various forms of enslavement were a general practice; like Catherine the Great's laws, which railroaded Russian people into serfdom. They applied to a new land their old way of thinking. Their religious intolerance was indistinguishable from that of England! We have people who insist they were bloody hypocrites. They were just a product of their time, like we are a product of ours. We had to wait until educated people, the Founding Fathers, for example, saw the opportunity that North America offered to build a new form of socio-political state. It takes time to build a nation, several centuries in fact.

BEFORE WE GO FURTHER, WE MUST CLARIFY OUR UNDERSTANDING OF FACTS AND SINS

We respect all people who are religious, it is their right and privilege; but our book is based on history and facts are not religious beliefs.

Mr. Dyson uses religiously charged words like innocence and guilt. It certainly exists and they are part of each human being's individual morality, but they should not be used to eliminate the concept of responsibility. For example: We dropped atomic bombs at the end of the second World War on Japan. We saved millions of lives, Japanese and American. Where is our guilt? The US had four options, was the right one chosen by President Truman. It is a matter of debate; was it morally wrong? Was it the right decision to save a lot of lives? Where is the sin? Well, we can tell that sin is in the act of war itself. It is appropriate to place the debate in a moral context as long as that isn't a way to avoid the basic consideration for real action, in a real world, where millions and millions of human lives could be lost.

DO WHITE PEOPLE OWE SOMETHING TO MINORITIES?

To all unhappy souls who are complaining about living in this country, let us spell out a few facts.

A 16-year-old young man who left his small hamlet in Poland, ended up in the Bronx with his wife, lived in a cramped tenement, worked all of his life, paid the university tuition of his two sons with cash saved in a cigar box (it was during the Great Depression of 1929), and both sons put their three children in college. Do you think that couple owes minorities something?

The young Irishman who arrived in Boston with his pregnant wife, couldn't find lodging in places where there were signs of "No dogs or Irish allowed" and then, since he was drafted right off the boat he had to fight for the Union in the Civil war--lost his life somewhere in the South. Was he under obligation to give money to Black people? His widow, who moved to New York, now worked as a cleaning lady, tithed to the Catholic Church to build St. Patrick's Cathedral, raised her kid, who grew up to be a cop, who had two children who rose to become professionals. Is she in debt to minorities?

And the Swedish people who settled in an area called the Badlands and made something of it, are they in hock to black minorities?

And the Chinese man buried in an unmarked grave along the railroad tracks that he built in the Northwest–does he have the obligations to pay something to black people?

And the Portuguese man who lost his life chasing whales for their precious oil lamps, does he or his family owe something to someone?

And what about the Latina, who lost her husband to disease, scraping by on an inhospitable minuscule piece of land to feed her family, does she have a tab with someone from a minority? Should we continue?

In this country nobody owes anything to anybody. We all came here, did all the crappy jobs, struggled, worked in horrible conditions. We, all of us, the Latino, the White, the Asians, the Blacks don't owe anything to anybody. We are asking here our fellow RRMs to "woke" from their deep ignorance of the history of this country and of the world if possible. It is fair for them to ask us to read *Black Boy*, by Richard Wright, but in return can they give other communities equal respect and read Upton Sinclair's *Jungle*, not to make them forget slavery, the misery, the suffering of the black community, but to understand that suffering is not exclusively the experience of the black people.

FREEDOM OF SPEECH AND POLITICAL CORRECTNESS

Disclosure: our group has less and less patience for people who spend an inordinate amount of time berating, admonishing, abusing and trying to silence people who do not share their opinion. We won't be muzzled by anyone. Don't try.

Political correctness has the support of many different groups. Some think it normal to charge twice as much to people based upon the color of their skin. That way of reasoning is a pure product of a collusion between political correctness and radical racist minorities. We do not think that replacing one form of racism by another is progress of any kind for a human society. Using the euphemism of non-POC (not a person of color) as a substitute for white is an example of the tartuffery, the bigotry of some people of color, since white is a color!

But know that a rapper, Jillian Grahan, aka 'Tiny Jag', canceled her participation to an AfroFuture musical festival, because she was "enraged" by the "non-progressiveness" and the "spite" from such politic. She is right; our future isn't in more ghettos, racism, prejudices, etc.

She did it in her own hometown and therefore we insisted, all along, that the issues aren't with minorities but inside their radical fringes which are out of control.

The RRMs on numerous college campuses censure speeches, peoples, movies, lectures etc. basically anything which doesn't reflect their opinions. We can see those violent 'leftist' groups everywhere now. We are the opposite kind of people; we drown bigotry, racism by our number. No violence to speak of, just a massive reprobation for intolerance. We didn't need baseball bats, guns, knives on the street of Skokie, IL, or on the streets of Boston, MA. We just stay on the sidewalk and let them know we disagree with them and it works!

But we have now more and more RRM who are aggressive and violent. They are the Alt-Left which quickly morphed into something where militants act like hoodlums, bullies with baseball bats, 3' metallic crow bars etc. They call themselves 'Anti-fa'(scist). Don't get fooled, they already are 'Fa-Anti-Fa' (Fascist-anti-fascist). It's easy to recognize them, they always hide their faces! [7]

They violently shut down the University of Kansas, a 1,000-person event on racism, because they didn't speak about it 'the right way'. They stopped the projection of a movie about the war in Iraq. They are ostracizing Chris Rock and Jerry Seinfeld, because they are too controversial. Seinfeld controversial? They must be kidding. Well, they aren't.

You can see the RRM at work in a video where a Yale professor, Nicholas Christakis, is encircled by an angry mob of students, insulting and asking for an apology because he said to "just look away" if you see an offensive Halloween costume! Or, about the President of

Evergreen, George Bridges, who was insulted in his office by some radicals who told him "to shut up," not to move his hands because they perceived it as threatening when he tried to give an answer, and who is "grateful" for the "passion and courage" demonstrated by that mob who took over the campus. It forced a professor, Brett Weinstein, to teach off-campus for safety reasons; that is fascism. It is worrisome when the leadership of some universities and colleges lack a sense of leadership, considering the poor example they show to students. [8]

Where are all the people from the 'Liberal left' who constantly chastise the citizenry, when democracy needs them? We are asking the ones with power, the 'Elite', who oversee our newspapers, the 'star' journalists, TV stations, the infosphere/media. They should have been up in arms and denouncing those people. Well, they didn't, and the question is why?

University of Chicago (UofC) has a pretty good grip on this situation. Geoffrey R. Stone, Professor of Law, created with some other faculty member, The U. of C. statement of Freedom of Expression (published in January 2015). It's a good document which can be used by all universities and colleges. Make students sign it, if they don't respect it, give them one or two warnings, and if they keep violating expel them. It's that simple. People are fed up hearing college undergraduates, chanting "My oppression is not a delusion." One of the characteristics of delusion is the unshakable belief that something is real when it is not. So, it is easy for them to see oppression in a college where you pay a $74,000 yearly tuition! Naturally, their self-pity is based on you and us being racist, homophobic, sexist, misogynistic etc. and them being victims. [9]

Academic and college administrations are in charge. It is the Higher Education's responsibility to spread ethics, leadership, ideals, morals, etc. and not to surrender their responsibilities to a bunch of narcissist morons. *"It is the obligation of Higher Education to defend Free Speech on their campus. If they refuse to do it, we must hold back financing from State and Federal sources until Laws of the Land are applied and respected. It is inadmissible that we can't express ourselves freely in our own country."* (USDF)

`We must defend the first Amendment on college and university campuses. If the RRM create trouble, let the campus police force handle them, and if they aren't strong enough, call the city police, if it is not enough, call the National Guard, not enough? Shut down the establishment if it is under thugs' control. We must make sure that everyone can say their piece. What are those radicals so afraid of? Some idiot spewing off some stupidities. Don't we already get it from them? Too many colleges/universities, are contributing passively to the emergence of an intolerant, highly politicized, dogmatic 'Elite' that we start to see everywhere in our administration as well as political parties and our judicial system. Our side of the political spectrum is appalled to see people claiming to be 'liberal left' acting in such a way that it reactivated the 'alt-right'. The latter always existed but had no recent major political impact to speak of. The constant censure on campus by RRM, gave the extreme right the pretext to reemerge as defenders of free speech.

We can't let the radical minorities triumph and impose their rules on the majority. It took only ten years for Hitler's thugs and cronies to take over Germany.

The political correctness movement is a political movement used by minorities like Badfem, Sexualists, RRM, Infosphere/owners who control the political discourse to their advantage. It started on campus, now it has spilled into the main culture and the street. "Whoever can control the street will one day control the State, for every form of power politics and a dictatorship-run state has its roots on the street." Joseph Goebbels.

Our Founding Fathers knew that when push came to shove only an armed citizenry will defend Freedom. We don't have that European tradition of masses going down the street to make government listen to them. Freedom of Speech, free Elections, Laws and Right to bear Arms must be in constant equivalence in our political system, and with our specific historical background, we can't afford to be defenseless when facing intolerant, racist, illiberal, sectarian, discriminatory people from any side of our political life.

Our group doesn't belong to any gun-toting faction. We are just concerned by the fact that violence is increasing rapidly in our society. We now have street manifestations without leadership to negotiate with the police. It means that anarchists are having a field day and doing whatever they want. Naturally, we have the usual incompetent idiots who are claiming to "defund the police"; so, self-defense is becoming an urgent necessity. Please, don't buy a gun if you don't intend to be trained and educated on how to own it. It isn't acceptable to see little or big shops in black neighborhoods being burned down or looted without letting people have the right to defend themselves and their property.

MR. DYSON HAS A "PLAN"
FOR WHITE PEOPLE

Let's go back to Mr. Dyson which represents the RRM's way of thinking. If you limit your knowledge to your own community you can end up with the 'Black victimhood' business plan, quite similar to the Badfem 'women victimhood'. It teaches whites to help the blacks, by buying a minority IRA (Individual Reparation Account). White people should also pay a secular tithe to help young black people. Does Mr. Dyson know that Latinos, Asians, and Native Americans weren't slaves. Some of them owned them, including some black people. Do these people have to pay reparations to the Black community?

So, Mr. Dyson, from George town University, has on his ledger 3 trillions of moneys due to the Black community; but he is overbid by Mr. William Darity and his wife, Kristen Millen, from Duke University, who want 12 Trillions. Well, if we follow their logic, they must give credit to public and private America who spent trillions and trillions to build housing, to support any group, association working on social injustice, free food stamps, Section 8, unemployment, Medicaid, financial help of all kinds, etc. They will have the obligation to adjust his accounting and we can't wait for the results. However, we agree with Mr. Dyson if he noticed that all aid distributed isn't done judiciously. One example is South-Central Los Angeles, where city hall gave billion after billion to different minorities' Administration, those who have very little to show for it.

Mr. Dyson and his friend's blackness arguments rest on the fact that only blacks are victims. The poorest are the Native, 0.7% of the population with 25% below poverty line. We will limit our conversation to the Radical Racist Minorities conundrum which can't face the fact that white is 60% to 75% of the population have numbering approximately 35 million in poverty. The RRM can paint most of them white to make them whiter if they want, they can even rub them with 'whiteness' and see if their privileges stick on their skin! All brainwashing won't change anything about their condition. We are concerned about all poor, not only the ones who are on a list of some racist militants. Being poor sucks! When a poor black women has ovarian cancer, it is certainly as dreadful for her as her poor white neighbor, who can't count on her knapsack full of whiteness, privileges and opportunity to get healthy since she can't afford any insurance!

The 'Victimhood Business Plan', aka the Black taxes, won't work because for too long we've seen a portion of the black community being by-passed by numerous other communities of color, who, after losing everything, came here without speaking our language, not knowing our alphabet, and were able to succeed. From the Iranian man opening an ice cream parlor, to the Vietnamese woman opening a Mani-Pedi parlor. Most of them used the school system to get an education. We know that any black family which focuses on education has access to the highest level of responsibility in this country. We aren't even speaking about President Obama, but Susan Rice, National Security Advisor, from a family where all five children attended college on a janitor's salary and a seamstress' income. The success of that family was based on values, work and personal talent; not on a song and dance called "Bad White People oh oh, so Racist, oh oh." [don't confuse her with Condoleeza Rice, Secretary of State of the Bush administration, also a very competent woman but from a different social background.]

If Martin Luther King couldn't convince the RRM of his own community of the power of education, what makes people think that anybody else can? We are convinced that the majority of African Americans understand that education and hard work are the road to success. But unfortunately, their voice is drowned in their extremist's rhetoric who choose to look anywhere else to confront the problems they are creating in their own community, they shouldn't forget the "it's not burn baby burn" it's 'learn, baby, learn." of MLK.

THE RESPONSIBILITY OF "DELUDED WHITE PEOPLE"

The RRM gets a lot of help from some white 'liberals' who feel guilty for whatever some people said to them they should feel guilty of. By now our readers know that we are much more interested in understanding the major social undercurrent that affects our lives than the self-indulgent discourse of people who are very careful to avoid dealing with tiresome problems like health care, housing etc. Their sanctimony and narcissism are engulfing us. They succumb to one's self-approval which contaminates our media.

Even an excellent journalist, with numerous awards to prove it, published, in the NYT, a series of columns titled "...Whites Just don't Get It." So, now by being from a white majority is the proof that you 'don't get it'? For us, it is just another example of the advance deterioration of that brand of 'liberalism' which finds it standard to write that much of the population is too stupid to understand something. Does that journalist feel sorry for the Asians who just don't get it? We think that some Asians just don't get it, like everybody else. The content of his articles isn't relevant, since 80% of newspaper readers glance only at the headlines.

Still, we have the obligation to reassure people by giving an example of why whites get it fine as well as black people. Both communities know that 89% of Blacks don't blame the sorry state of some Black families on Whites who 'don't get it'; but on, what the NYT of September 10, 2017 wrote, that "on average, early childhood education reduces the kindergarten black-white achievement gap by nearly 50%." There is nothing wrong with Black families except that too many are mono-parental. Not because there is something wrong with black men but because some are poorly educated and unable to be employed. They won't find a good, stable job, which is the minimum requirement to assume basic social responsibilities. It is impossible to care for a family with two children on a Burger King salary. It is very upsetting for the citizenry which, for decades after decades, begged our Party to create a unify day care system, a real education apparatus and never getting it because of the usual excuse of lack of funds. So, to see Mr. Chuck Schumer bringing with the snap of his finger, 350 Billion as a down payment, for probably the 3 to 12 Trillion, as a repair for slavery, a few months before a presidential election is gut-churning to us who asked, for decades, that amount of money to rebuild our Public School system which will be greatly beneficial to the less fortunate. It's appalling to buy votes that way.

Therefore, Blacks in need are talking about day-care system, kindergarten, early education here and we can guarantee to all our deluded white liberals we all 'get it'. History, here again, shows decades of racists trying everything they could to keep, not only blacks, but all lower social stratas from getting a good education. The problem isn't based on color but on access to education which is the major threat to any ruling interests anywhere in the world. *"Education is the best way to knock out the good old 'Domination to Control and Exploit' (D.C.E.)."* (USDF) It's not by accident that, after the Civil War, the leadership of the Confederation made sure the Reconstruction laws kept education separated.

Radicals continue to disregard the fundamental fact that the social differences between groups are mostly based, in the modern world, on one's position on the economic ladder. It is well established that power exists due to the size of your wallet rather than the color of your skin. Are we supposed to be equal? Yes, and we are, except that rich people are more equal than others, aren't they? Are Jay-Z and Beyoncé equal to the mid-Western white couple with three kids whose mother is waitressing at Joe's coffee shop and whose father's working at WalMart as a security guard? What does the color of their skin mean? Absolutely nothing! Jay Z and Beyoncé aren't 'victims', and the couple from the Mid-West aren't 'privileged'.

A little break from serious matters:

The 'whiteness privilege theory' doesn't do very well with somebody like Tiger Woods who defined himself as a Cablinasian since his father is African American, Chinese and Native American and his mother is Thai, Chinese and of Dutch descent. What does that mean? It means that everybody is just f......g everybody, and that the race concept is just a political tool for racists on all sides.

THE IMPORTANCE OF HISTORY

Disclosure: Some opportunists will tell you that journalism or sociology are history; no, they aren't. Both are very useful in their own discipline. Some crafty rascals always try to bulk their ideas, research, political opinion, militancy with history, mainly to hide how shakily anemic their ideas are. [10] The ones to specially watch out for are the revisionists historians' work framed only to fit their opinions. But good historical fiction books can give readers great enjoyment and we highly recommend them.

As George Orwell said, "the most effective way to destroy people is to deny and obliterate their own understanding of their history."

"for this bright
morning dawning for you.
History, despite its wrenching pain,
cannot be unloved, but if faced
with courage, need not to be lived again
give birth again
to the dream."
"On the pulse of morning"
Maya Angelou poem for Barack Obama Presidential inauguration.

"History is intrinsic to establishing a people identity." (USDF)

In this paragraph we remind people that history isn't a cemetery to hang out, but a dynamic device to understand our present and shape the future. It is not the same as the past we can't experience. We are too late, it's gone, and people are buried. History is important because we can reconstruct it, with limited apparatus for sure, but still learn from it.

It is a research tool which helps our understanding of the past and consequently the present. It is never a creed of death, longing for the good old times, or as a refuge to justify the present from the injuries of the past. We assess the facts of the past to build the future. All human experience happens in a frame of historical reference which can make us grasp who they were and who we are.

Nonetheless, our Western Civilization has a very strong sense of historical dynamism at its core. It is the combination of Greek philosophy (rational thinking) and Christianity, which teach us to dominate (control) nature (not to destroy it!), by reason of humans not created by nature but by God. It is a fundamental difference with the Extreme Oriental Pantheism (creation/symbiosis with nature). The Western understanding of human history is completely separated from the reality of nature.

For the best and the worst, history is a human business. It created an historical dynamism in the Western Civilization, which gave us a sense of anticipation of the future because we, not only can compare the past with the present, but from there we can project a future. We all are "characters and agents of history" (Reinhold Niebuhr). But it's not a simple issue since humans, being what they are, rarely acknowledge that their ambitions, their most secret desires, their determination, their greed, their lust, their ambition alters their way of thinking rationally!

Unfortunately, we are facing now a de-historization of our society, not from a brutal dictatorship, but from the impact of the infosphere/media which brings a massive volume of information which is manufactured as historical facts. One of the consequences is that it fractures the social discourse with a cacophony of words and images thrown at us without any filter, logic, or socio-historical coherence. It is very bad because it drastically lowers our capacity to understand the functional rationality behind all social undertakings. *"Too many people now live in a present without historical depth. They are weightless, floating around in the raft of their emotions, left out from the knowledge of what their society is."* (USDF) If people like Hitler, Stalin, Pol Pot, Mao-Tse-Dong etc. tried to erase history and rewrite it on piles of dead human bodies, they certainly had some reasons—however nefarious.

So, the control of history is a highly human and political issue. It helps us to apprehend 'facts' in their context. Only a combination of historical knowledge and enlightenment can create the fertile ground for social progressivism and its values. The RRM is using facts from the past to justify the present - using the tools and values of today. This is an aberration! You must write and talk about the past using the cultural tools of the past. Otherwise you can't understand why the Aztecs sacrificed people to make sure the sun rises the following day. *"The RRM are hanging for too long in the Cemeteries of the past, they aren't into History, they are into necrophilia."* (USDF)

HISTORY, EDUCATION AND POLITIC

Education should be the first concern to all of us, because when people are educated, they succeed to their capacity--it is that simple. So, let's look at some numbers: From 2006 to 2016, total enrollment, after post-secondary in undergraduate, graduate and professional school increased by a total of 11.7%, Hispanic enrollment increased by 80.6 %, Black 15.4%, Asian, Pacific Islander, Native Hawaiian etc. 17.4%, White decreased by 5.2%. [11] An 11.7% increase even if it is progress is much too low and to slow to resolve any problems. We must show some incompetent leaders that their politics are wrong. They keep unqualified teachers in the school system, because salaries of teachers help their families to survive and not end up on welfare. Perhaps their intentions are good, but it is in fact catastrophic for their future. When Chicago had to close 44 schools -yes 44- because of their absurdly low level of education, they were just warehousing generation after generation of young people who didn't get any training or education for employment. We will find a lot of those young people full of energy, without any decent future, in the South Side trying to make it in some illegal business which need the use of a lot of guns. They don't know how to use and certainly didn't buy it in a store. It shouldn't have happened that a black woman cooking the dinner, with her daughter doing her hone work on the kitchen table, heard a noise of broken glass, turned her head and see her child pouring blood over her home work because she got a lost bullet in her head. It's not racism which is responsible for her death it is the decades of very low level of education. We must connect the dots!

As soon as one school is below any standard of education agreed on, the county, city hall, the State must move on to that issue. We know that some neighborhoods have a very low cultural tradition. Therefore, we suggest having an educational system which supersedes that situation by making sure from the earliest age that children are in and stay in school. It will protect them, partially for sure, from their environment; but at least we will offer them a way out of it. We must keep children of the street, by giving them the opportunity to do their homework in the safe environment of the school, where older students will give them tutoring, etc. After recess or sport activities, a snack will be welcome. A reading room is easy to set up and can be available until parents come to get them. Any suggestion would be better than to kick children out of school at 2:30 or 3:00 pm and let them hang out on the street to be easy prey for all the creeps. We already have the infrastructure. Let's keep schools open late. We are talking about re-orienting an extensive part of our education system. We know for a fact that a lot of competent leaders from minorities agree with us. We don't have that many tools available at the federal level, to revamp, make headway in making our society livable; but education is one of them.

WHITENESS PART 2

It is an offspring of a combination of post-modernism and historicism–historismus.[12] It is an interpretation of history through literature, poetry, songs--everything cultural. Berkeley University of 1970 was the beacon for that kind of culture. Camille Paglia assumed our opinion very well by calling "the intellectual humanities production from that university crap." [13]

But, still, what is it in 2020? We have now a shared new concept between racist radical minorities, Badfem, and sexualists but, "..,whiteness is hard to pinpoint (here again, like feminism, what is it?) there is a widespread agreement (from whom) that whiteness (you mean like yellowness, blackness, brownness?) is a social construct (by whom?) that is normalized (how?) as a system of privilege (for a few or everybody?)" All parentheses are ours. These are the words of Ruth Frankenberg, sociologist. She builds her 'whiteness theory' on 30 in-depth interviews of white women, which is now plenty enough for BadAcademia, to build a political movement! [14]

First, it is now a trademark of these intellectuals to avoid any clear definition of what they are talking about; because that way they can feed the public an insane amount of futile, pointless ideas, lies and exaggerations, that our group calls bullshit!

Second, if you replace "whiteness" by "women" it could have been lifted verbatim out of the Badfem playbook, so, nothing new here.

Third, any verbal nonsense must be paid respect since it is coming from some university's radical humanities departments. Well we, us, our group don't genuflect in front of any intellectual jabber from anybody.

Fourth, Whiteness exists only because infosphere/media disseminates and propagates such blither. It isn't a scientific, historic or philosophic postulation. It is a tentative way to create a theory from assumption--speculation based on beliefs, opinions, individual viewpoints.

It's a pure product of bad historicism!

Let's quickly look at a potpourri of quotes found everywhere in the media. The Critical Whiteness Study -CWS- by the Oxford Research, Critical Whiteness Study is also a very useful source.

The whites must learn to acknowledge, rather than deny, how they are complicit in racism.

White supremacy is to race what patriarchy is to gender.

What privilege looks like to a broke white person... is different from what privilege looks like to Donald Trump. Nevertheless, even if experienced differently, all white people in some way benefit from whiteness.

Whites are carrying a knapsack of privileges.

An invisible system of white norms is the condition of racialism.

All those affirmations desperately need an intellectual seal of approval. The more abstruse or complex the better it is, because who is going to start a discussion about Edmund Husserl, Hume, or Merleau-Ponti's work? Philosophy is a very serious discipline, but Badfem are going to borrow language from serious philosophy for their discourse. Unfortunately, too many good people believe they must accept what they say because nobody understands what they mean. Irving Howe, in Harper's Magazine, described them as "a figment of the Zeitgeist, bearing the rough and careless marks of what is called higher education and exhibiting a talent for the delivery of gross simplicities in tones of leaden complexity."

FATUOUS CONFUSION BETWEEN BIAS, PREJUDICE AND RACISM BY HARVARD

We have the interesting case of the I.A.T., Implicit Association Test, better known as "Implicit Bias". It is a test that the media seized upon and informed us it was of great significance. Finally, we had a test that would tell us that we are racist. That test was introduced 20 years ago by two researchers Nahzarin Banaji, chair of Harvard University psychology department, and Anthony Greenwald, researcher at the University of Washington. Based on their data they concluded that 95% of people are biased. What a gold mine for the RRM people, who could use the study to justify their politics. For twenty years we were submerged by articles and interviews ad nauseum; proving beyond a shadow of a doubt that we are racially biased, meaning racist. The American Psychological Society Magazine wrote that the IAT test was "A revolution in social psychology".

OOPS! When the re-testing was done, the IAT didn't pass the test of minimum reliability, meaning it's well below any usefulness for any society. Harvard University opened a website where you could take that test. Over 17 million people did!

Let's see the consequences of chowing down for twenty years that kind of idiocy from Harvard, propagated by the media.

Researchers must re-adjust the results of their work to sustain and improve it. But for twenty years the authors never published anything of that sort. It is a minimum requirement if you want to label your work 'scientific'. Otherwise it is like Ford Motor Company selling you a car in 2018 that is the same as the one in

1998! Let's look at the test itself.

Like all tests it shows that if you change, however slightly, the wording of a question, the results will change.

The test doesn't predict a discriminatory behavior at all! You have the example of a cultured pharmacist who took the test, only to discover that he was biased against brown and Muslim people. He was surprised to read this given that he was Brown and Muslim!

During those twenty years, much scholarly work was done to alert academia as well as the public of the deficiency of that test. Let's name a few of those researchers, Philip Tetlock, Wharton School professor, very well known in behavioral sciences, Hart Blanton, University of Connecticut, Gregory Mitchell, UVA school of Law, Hal Markets of Ohio State University, James Jaccard of NYU.

And this is our question: Why didn't Harvard University notify the media that there was a problem with the study?

We don't blame the media for not having an opinion on an academic issue; we are blaming the media for not keeping us informed when there are some serious issues with that study. It is the job of journalists to continue to follow the subjects they choose to investigate and write about.

By not doing their job, academia and the media let the RRM, sexualists and Badfem use flawed research to build racist arguments against most people; they falsely equate bias with racism and prejudice.

The fact is, there is no causal relationship between bias and racism. Some black people aren't racist because they don't like pop music, neither do white people when they dislike rap. If Asians are biased against Wagner it doesn't mean they are racist! Whites, blacks, Asians, browns all have proclivity based on their culture and not on the color of their skin; racism has nothing to do with it.

But now let's look at how RRM use these notions. Katherine Kirkenes, mental health counselor and doctorate fellow at SUNY Albany and Sarah Birdsong, mental health counselor and emotional intelligence educator opened a business since they "... have a scientific way to train white people to stop being racist". They offer their service to corporations because they can fire up their employees to talk about racism and "When that happens, all emotional hell breaks loose because they (only white people, of course) just don't have the tolerance to deal with it, and, depending on their personality, tend to either erupt or shut-down." Meaning, white people kill themselves or 'go postal' on their colleagues. The ones who are laughing their heads off are minorities, since almost all the latest are instigated by them!

Our readers can have a pretty good idea of the intellectual level of the whiteness crowd by reading, on qz.com, April 11, 2016, K. Kirkenes's article about how to train white people. Please, don't miss the picture chosen to illustrate that article. This is how the RRM see white people. It's hilarious because she is serious in her intent.

Still, don't underestimate those two white ladies; it is a brilliant business plan to make money. Corporations will hire them just to protect themselves in case of lawsuits, which invariably happen when an employee gets passed over for a promotion and cries racism or harassment because of the gaze of their supervisor. (All quotes above are public knowledge.)

Fredrick Douglass, in 1892-1893, wrote that science wasn't the antidote of white people's racism. There is no scientific validity whatsoever in any theories based on race and science, <u>they all end up in racism.</u> Trivia question for our RRM: who wrote "racism is racism; no matter what the color, the racist is voicing the ugly words." (see ADDENDUM)

We need to sum up here the last three chapters, before we address the bone of contention American people have with GAFAMEDFI.

The most dangerous evolution of our political life is for us to witness that the coalition of Badfem, sexualists and radical minorities, not able to win popular vote, use the judicial to advance their claims. They are displacing the political power in such a way that we will end up being governed by laws instead of elected people, so no more check and balance in our political system. Their political irresponsibility blind them to the fact that democracy is the form of government which protects them. Remove democracy and they are opening the door to any kind of autocratic, theocratic, ethnocratic form of government which will get rid of them and their claims in a second when useless. *"They all lost the cognition, the meaning of the totemic symbol of one people, one flag, one anthem, which all are essential as myths to forge, in our case a democratic nation and unify a social reality called America"*. (USDF) Most people from our group think they are too far out and lost for the good left. They are addicted to their clique's dogmas. What can we do? We wish all of them good luck and they must get out of the progressive left that they are using shamelessly. They shouldn't forget to take with them their 2019 "Babushka look" from the fashion runways.

NOTES

1. Scientists find DNA differences between gay men and their straight twin brothers, (see latimes.com, Oct. 8, 2015. Article based on UCLA Molecular biologist Tuck C. Nugget researches

2. see Ayn Rand's philosophy is extremely elitist, and a man should be concerned "...with his own happiness as the moral purpose of his life..." Atlas Shrugged, appendix, June 14, 2010

3. quotes from: The Munk debates of 2018.

4. Adrienne Lafrance, The Intolerant Left, The Atlantic, Nov. 14, 2017

5. New York Time Magazine, Nov.26, p. 34, 2017

6. smithsonianmag.com, the Misguided Focus on 1619 as the Beginning of the Slavery in the US Damages our Understanding of America History

7. Eoin Lenihan, It's Not Your Imagination: The Journalists Writing About Antifa Are Often Their Cheerleaders, Quillette.com, May 29,2019

8. Bradford Richardson, Spineless Evergreen State College President Express "Gratitude" for Students who Took Over Campus, The Washington Times, Monday, May 21, 2017

9. Heather Mac Donald, Why Are Colleges Students So Afraid of Me? WSJ, Nov. 26, 2019

10. A good example of how history can be manipulated is exposed in Gertrude Himmelfarb, One Nation, Two Cultures, A Searching Examination of American Society in the Aftermath of our Cultural Revolution, Vintagebooks, January 2012

11. U.S. Department of Education, integrated postsecondary Education Data System, 2016. The Chronicle of Higher Education, September 28, Section B, P.B-34.
12. see Karl W.F. Schlegel in Wikipedia-
13. see also Karl R.Popper, The Poverty of Historicism, Routledge & Kaplan, 1960.)
14. White Women, Race Matters, The Social Construction of Whiteness, chapter, White on White p. 27, she wrote that some were feminist, lesbian, middle class, from poor background, Marxist-Leninist etc. all living in Santa Cruz or San Francisco
15. Merleau-Ponti, quoted by Sara Ahmed, Phenomenology of Whiteness, Goldsmiths College, University of London
16. A very good definition of phenomenology can be found in, stanford.edu/entries/phenomenology/ David Carr, Experience and History: Phenomenological Perspectives on Historical World, Oxford University Press. Sara Ahmed, A Phenomenology of Whiteness, Feminist Theory 2007, 8:18 149, sagepub.com/content/8/2/149. You also can find some of her work on dadadocot.com. Barbara Applebaum, Being White, Being Good: White Complicity, White Moral Responsibility, and Social Justice Pedagogy, Lexington Books, 2011. Robin DiAngelo, Privilege and Politic, grad.uw.edu, October 26, 2016. Her white fragility theory could be entertaining as an example of Bad Academia. For example: "I don't believe it's humanly possible to be free of bias."! See below.

INFOSPHERE / MEDIA

"The really frightening thing about totalitarianism is not that it commits 'atrocities' but that it attacks the concept of objective truth; it claims to control the past as well as the future." George Orwell

"One of the saddest lessons from history is this: If we have been bamboozled long enough, we tend to reject any evidence of bamboozle. We're no longer interested in finding out the truth. The bamboozle has captured us. It's simply too painful to acknowledge, even to ourselves, that we have been taken. Once you give a charlatan power over you, you almost never get it back." Carl Sagan, from The Demon-Haunted World: Science as a Candle in the Dark.

"Where the press is free, and every man able to read, all is safe." Thomas Jefferson

"Information is light. Information, in itself, about anything, is light." Tom Stoppard

TO INTRODUCE THAT chapter let's look at two examples of basic manipulations of the citizenry by the media.

In the New Yorker, Elizabeth Kolbert wrote an article about "who owns the internet?" [1] The author gave us a sample of how on November 7, 1876, Rutherford B. Hayes was convinced he was losing the presidential election and that his opponent, Samuel J. Tilden, would be the next president, but Tilden lost! Hayes was elected thanks to manipulation by the Associated Press with the help of Western Union who muted news that favored Tilden. This offers a glimpse of how, if a century and half ago, people were able to double cross the voters during an election, and that without the help of the Russians! Manipulation of the electoral process, by a foreign power is small potatoes compared to what owners of our infosphere/media complex can do.

Another good illustration of that power is Gary Hart's 1988 presidential run, torpedoed when he was the front runner. Some good old boy from the Republican Party fabricated an affair, which allegedly never happened, between a young woman and that candidate. It was the media which made that complot succeed.

The three previous chapters were about the Badfem, sexualists and radical minorities that we regrouped now into a global RRM system, which have for a goal to dismantle our foundational values as they are an obstacle to their ambitions. The core of it rests on their communitarian politic which breeds and propagates social differences to an extent that it locks groups of people into ghettos. Numerous existed before and where the substructure of Irish, Latinos, Jews, etc. communities.

Cinque De Mayo, Sunday School, Kwanza festivities, food festivals, the Ukrainian's folkloric groups or the carol singing groups never affected the cohesion of our nation. So why are some small communities able to now change the laws in our country? How come their perverted, distorted, gnarled commentaries can pollute our society with so much divisiveness? They would have remained little, noisy groups if they didn't get massive help from people who see all the political advantages, they might get from them. The question is why did the RRM end up on the laps of the Neo-Liberal SuperCapital? Well, the latest need the RRMs, the "useful idiots," to deconstruct, denature our value system which are an obstacle to implement their economic theories, which cover up their economic interests. Let's look at how the infosphere/media engages in that process. (see ADDENDUM)

HOW INFOSPHERE/MEDIA COMPLEX EMERGED

We need to be specific in this chapter. We aren't writing about Juan Carlos Huerta or Javier Valdez from Riodoce newspaper. The latest was gunned down, because they were doing their jobs reporting on the horror of the "Narco guerra civil" in Mexico. Or about Jamal Khashoggi cut in little pieces in Istanbul Saudi's consulate, or any good journalist working on informing us about the turpitude and corruption in our political apparatus, or the one working in the food, fashion, sports, technology etc. field. From all over the world, they try to inform us about the pleasant and not-so-serious fact of life but also about the injustice, the violence, the stupidity so common in any human society. Most of the time they are poorly paid and are in a very precarious social position. We are much more worried about the minority who alter our perception of reality since they are part of the transmission belt which carries the ideological themes and goals of the few MegaCorps who own them.

We are facing now a general mistrust of the media by the public, which is dealing constantly with misinformation, smears, half-truths, manipulations of all kinds daily. There are no more facts but "alt-facts" and buckets of opinions, ideological gospel from the pens of editors in chief and their journalists, pundits of any kind etc. There is no exchange of ideas, no back and forth of arguments, no significant political debates, just a ton of mud slide. *"It is really bad, because all of us are swimming now in a media-sea of fatuousness, just fragments of squabbles, floating about."* (USDF) It is ludicrous to expect the American people to make sense of such a meaningless stew.

So, for us 'facts' are becoming of primordial importance since 'truth' is eviscerated by people who think there is no truth but opinion in it. It is an outcome of post-modernism theory which explains that sorry state of affairs in the information kingdom. In this paragraph we will pay a lot of attention to how 'facts' are handled by the infosphere. We certainly don't intend to accept their opinion as truth.

Modern infosphere/media rest on a technological revolution which brought us fantastic and exceptional tools called the computer, Internet, websites etc. We are big fans of it; there are no Luddites among us. It originated with the US Army, which wanted to connect all its computers. Higher education establishments like MIT, Stanford, Harvard, A&M etc. under the patronage of the US Government who financed with generous grants this research, are now owned or controlled by a few giant conglomerates. All those GAFA and numerous others, are a product of that time. The finance people came with the money necessary to extend it to the planet. That's all good news. Giant corporations certainly can bring progress. But our MegaCorp owners understood very quickly that those new tools could also be awesome instruments to control and bend our social discourse, to an extent never seen before. It was relatively easy since they finance the structure which carries it.

So, let's stop for a while all the OOhs and AAhs from the infosphere, about the wonder of neo-liberalism.

We must stick to the ground and look at the mudslide, which existed before, escalate drastically when an old, more or less, independent media structure collapsed into the fold of a much larger system of propagation of information called the infosphere which is based on high-tech and economic concentration that had a huge impact on how we are informed. It started with

President Reagan's 1996 deregulation of the telecommunication business which opened enormous business opportunities for everybody; it had a positive effect on our economy by creating enough room for an onslaught of high-tech start-ups. But it also put in place the conglomeration of the media business by removing the cap of ownership of radio stations, right to own 4 TV stations in the same market, etc. But President Clinton reinforced that tendency with his "Digital Media Act" of 1996.

It did exactly the opposite. It created giant corporations where there were none! In 1983 we had around 50 interest groups, controlling the news, now we have 5 or 6. Those enormously powerful MegaCorps, would not miss the opportunity to add television networks, newspapers, Hollywood studios, publishing companies, newspapers etc. to their portfolio. This offered them a tremendous political ascendency given the control infosphere/media has over our socio-political discourse.

But why such a blunder from a sophisticated Democrat President? Did he forget how capitalism works? Its natural tendency is to concentrate, to gobble up everything which can increase its power. President Clinton was the first one to know how critical the media are to win an election and to influence the social discourse. Did anybody in the Democratic Party see how dangerous these deregulations were? It's certainly not easy to know in advance the impact of a new law, but why wasn't the law recalled after it became clear it was having such detrimental impact on our democracy. It is the job of our political party to make sure democracy is always protected. They failed and didn't protect information from SuperCapitalism.

But what we now have is a president who can reach out directly to the citizenry through tweets (little gadget pure product of the infosphere), by-passing entirely the traditional medias.

But it doesn't explain why President Trump's tweets were making the news. Why are the daily, 140-character reactions of someone, even a President reducing political debate? Why were the media playing with his cards? They had the choice of answering with sensible political choice from any political party. Or even not to answer tweets from anybody! If someone disagrees with the building of a wall South of the border, we must have our own proposals to offer to the citizenry, don't we? A Democrat Congresswoman going to the border and trying to bring into the country illegal immigrants isn't a political proposal. It's some flashy, political opportunism for media consumption. We don't expect any progress from that kind of jesting.

Is it the access of a mass of people and organizations which created that meaningless media chatter system? Is it the massive amount of raw information thrown at us? The impact of numeric big data? Does it have something to do with the concentration of ownership?

Well, it's none of the above! Our party has been unable to formulate any coherent immigration politic for quite a while.

THE PRINTED PRESS:

When Arthur Sulzberger Jr, publisher of The New York Times, told students at Columbia School of Journalism, (New York, April 6, 2011) that "he wants to give information of quality to a public of quality," what does that mean exactly? Because we have the unpleasant feeling that our newspapers think and treat us like people, not of quality, but as a bunch of pathetic idiots. So, what is a public of quality? The cultivated class? The people in or close to any form of power? The educated, aloof upper-class? Lacking a clear understanding of what Mr. Sulzberger meant won't stop us from writing about a certain number of problems we have with our NYT and the media in general. We are from the discerning left, and we don't understand why our main newspaper, after winning so many Pulitzer prizes, does such a poor job at informing its public about truth—what's really happening politically in the US. As we said, we do not consider comment on a president's tweets as political information, neither is the constant pandering to trendy causes.

Mr. Sulzberger isn't some Super villain of the media sphere. We can read from Mr. Marc fisher, senior editor, and Sydney Trent, a journalist from the Washington Post, a spiteful, dreadful, piece about a woman who dare to wear a costume that Lexie Gruber and Lyric Prince, didn't apparently understand as a parody and that during a private Halloween party. We are dealing here with not only stupidity, but viciousness. *"Time is ripe for systematically expose all those 'yellow pigs' for what they are, offspring of the crass yellow press from England"* (USDF) A thank you note to The-American-Interest.com/2020/06/28 for making us aware of that story.

To criticize a president, or any president is totally fine with us, but 24/7/365 political lynching is not. By doing so, aren't we just hiding the hollowness of our own politic? The NYT's obsession with the "huge scandal of Stormy Daniel's" encounter with our president make the journalists look like Kenneth Starr's team. [2] Obsessing over the details of what was a banal sexual encounter between adults, that should have been resolved by the first family privately. It is not the job of the press. Making fun of a president non-stop is entertainment; that's Colbert's, Conan's, Fallon's, Kimmel's etc. job, not the NYT.

We read too many articles that reflect the bias and prejudice of the journalists or editors. Let's give our readers just a few samples of their work. [3]

First, a piece about a woman who served as Korean President. During her tenure, a scandal erupted because she consulted a Shaman woman as an advisor on state matters and both were cashing in on it. The furor of the people from South Korea was justified. On the street, as many women as men protested, demanding her resignation. [4] The NYT's journalist asked her American readers what role sexism and misogyny played in the termination of her presidency. That presidential policy was anti-union, corrupted to the bones. She was effectively pulling her country several centuries back in time when the future was read in tea leaves! She was sentenced to 32 years in jail, no less! Does the redactor in chief have anybody around to catch this kind of ludicrous narrative of sexism and misogyny, born from Badfem persuasion? People can ask, isn't she just one journalist among many? Yes, she is, but eight years later we still read the same line of reasoning in our newspaper.

Second piece, in the frontpage of NYT Sunday, August 11, 2019 we read, Many Gunmen in Mass Shooting Share a Hate Toward women. It's a long article explaining that the common thread between most of mass shootings is misogyny. They use incidents from the murderer's past, domestic violence, divorce, a misogynistic viewpoint on the Internet to sustain their arguments.

We are surprised that those journalists didn't notice that people on a collision course with their own suicide/death aren't especially all goody-goody with their environment! We see here the use of a word which means first hatred of women, (Cambridge English Dictionary, Merriam Webster, etc.) contempt and prejudice. By using it they give credit to that absurd Badfem's claim that mass murderers are one of the expressions of hatred among American men toward women. That's just cretinous. But it is certainly not that ridiculous since you find that word everywhere, at every corner of our leftist social discourse.

Are these journalists lazy? Can't they express their opinions without referring constantly to buzzwords like sexism, misogyny, patriarchy, that we are defining in our lexicon? Are they victims of political correctness which imposes a codified language? We didn't ask, but our concern is that they give too much broad credit to the idea of hatred in our society. That a bunch of Viciousfem use it, fine, we know who they are, but to find it in the NYT? By not doing its job, it dodges crucial issues much more important than Badfeminism propaganda. May we suggest the disappearance of most public mental health facilities? Please don't serve us Badfem propaganda; it's offensive.

Third piece is about racism: Let's look at a front-page article, "Trump Turns to Old Tactic: Using Race for His Gain," NYT, Sunday, July 21, 2019. It is a long article about President Donald Trump's "racism." They are free to say whatever they want, but they, OUR journalists have the obligation to let their readers know that racism is also all over our side. They mention Tawana Brawley from thirty years ago. But they disregard Jussie Smollett from yesterday! They ignored the outrage of Chicago's black leaders, from the mayor to the police chief, appalled by the tricks used by a third-rate actor in need of publicity. Those leaders ask for everything except to have some moron pouring gasoline on racial issues. Chicago has so many real problems to take care of. Are the NYT people blind to the point of not seeing "whiteness" theory as a race card when the authors of it, *the RRM themselves, say it is!* What else do those journalists need or want? Why do they refuse to give us the full picture is the question? Do they think their readers aren't noticing it? Do they think we are stupid?

Racism from either side is not acceptable. The consequences of letting a newspaper choose RRM's "good" racism" is likely to increase it throughout society.

These few examples above enable us to understand that we don't get any "...information of quality for a public of quality." *"Even if they are a minority, we have too many unprincipled, deceitful reporters who now realize they have the power to make any events appear legitimate without commitment to reality. They don't need the latest since the infosphere gives that legitimacy by mouthing, echoing, ranting on the opinions of any journalist."* (USDF) Those people are very useful to propagate any kind of disinformation. It doesn't mean that in the same journal you don't have excellent reporters, doing a first-class job. But those will work on the Weinstein affair, not on the collusion between SuperConglos and mass media. [5]

IT IS THE SAME ALL OVER SOCIETY

Too many people use 'Freedom of the Press' as a shield. But it doesn't give the right to publish knowingly truncated facts. Does it? Can the press strengthen and increase their fact checking departments, instead of making them smaller? If they don't, soon the press will become just one more foghorn of noise in our already cacophonous society and the First Amendment will die of natural causes since we won't have any freedom of the press to defend it!

For us, the real danger is the phenomenon of obscuration of facts._Many journalists aren't in the 'Truth' business, (that's a scary thought!) They must report to the public, facts as clearly and honestly as they can. They certainly have the right to comment on it. But what we are getting instead are reporters who judge, explain and give their interpretation on cherry picked snippets of facts, used only to confirm the opinions of the person who wrote or published it. But by manipulating facts they manipulate the 'Truth' that all of us try to establish for ourselves. How can we establish a cogent, insightful opinion of our perception of reality,_since the infosphere/media refuse to give us facts–only but their interpretation of it? [6] By not clearly separating facts from opinions they can always wedge opinions over facts. *"The danger is real when we see everywhere a submission of our intellectual life to a formatting by infosphere/media. Naturally some people are cringing, crawling at the feet of the infosphere/media, to be seen on TV."* (USDF) This is one of the roots of why we are, as a nation, less intelligent than 30 years ago.

The readers can be easily convinced by following the political debates of the 2020 democratic primaries. How embarrassing was it to see all our candidates speaking over each other, raising their arms like little schoolchildren trying to get the attention of teachers. The media people, CBS in this case, did a very good job at making them look ridiculous. They could have put on each lectern a button telling them they must push it to request a time for answer. The journalists could have requested a switch on their side to turn off the microphone of the repeated offenders of speaking over the arguments of another candidate. This is another example of how primeval it is to the infosphere/media complex to revamp everything as diversion, divertissement etc. Our group certainly enjoyed from unreasonable to idiotic entertainment but at the level of a presidential debate, it is alarming and scary.

"SUBLIMINAL MESSAGES" AREN'T HARMLESS

They are in pictures, advertising, movies, newspaper, speeches; we choose a few low keys on purpose. We want to show that the hidden content has in fact a deep impact on our daily life.

Those pieces of information are directed at consumers to make them buy a product, but when you look at it closely, you realize that many carry a socio-political message. Tom Ford's company advertised their shoes with explicit pictures. The ad in question shows a woman on her back. Of course, she is gorgeous, but has the stiletto of another women, deep in her throat. The Lesbian-Sado-Masochist content of that image is quite evident. It is a take-off from an advertisement published in E.U. during the '70s. It represented also a woman's head, but this time sticking her tongue out to reach the tip of her lover's stiletto. The theme of lesbianism was certainly present, but no violence to speak of. In the US, the image now is filled with violence which the advertising business traffics in.

When we walk on the street we don't try to interpret or analyze a photo. But there are consequences for our absorption of daily violence under the cover of selling a pair of shoes. Let's take another example from the same company. This time we see a long-legged model running scared, in the middle of a road, pursued very closely by a Rolls Royce driven by a white man, his white skin and red hair makes certain that you don't miss that point, leaning menacingly on his steering wheel. He certainly wants to run over the woman. But why advertise a blue miniskirt and a light blue shiny top with such a dramatic and violent subtext? Well, people, it serves to reinforce the so called rage of white men over women (misogyny anybody?); 90% of people walking on the street won't pay attention to it, still our brains will notice; and it will reinforce the socio-political noise of "female victimhood." Through advertising we receive a negative and vicious message of the nature of our society. TV advertising also conveys a negative even racist message. It is a mistake to think it is just a flickering on our retina. It's printed in our memory bank.

But what about the repercussions on our pre-pubescent 6- to 15-year-old daughters and sons, who are exposed to these images as well. Our little girl will learn that women must run to escape a menacing big car driven by a white man, and the little boy will think that when you have a big car there's nothing awful about running after women with it. Well, isn't this a way to prepare them to accept violence between men and women as just another fact in our society? It is certainly acceptable if it is in plain sight on the street?

We all are horrified by how violent our society has become. Well, it didn't come from nowhere. It's nested in our socio-economic and political culture. But why is the media reinforcing this brutishness to the point of obscenity? The ferocity of the economic competition in the fashion business does not justify Tom Ford's viciously sadistic advertising. Violence, cruelty, brutality is now everywhere, in cartoons for children, video games for teenagers, TV shows, advertising, movies, sports. It looks like people in charge want to convince us that it is a shared value between all of us. We don't think so, because only a tiny fraction of lesbians is involved in this kind of extreme sexual practice; and still, millions of people saw that advertising, attempting to convince them that it is so mainstream that you can find it on the street, meaning misogyny is a massive social reality when it isn't. The fact that some men are misogynist doesn't justify advertising misogyny as a global social reality. The media complex is replacing our real world with its own version of it. It is the same social manipulation denounced by the Goodfem, about the absurd representation of the female body in all those women's magazines. We certainly have the right to do something about it. Interestingly, the LHBTQ+++ is not protesting at Tom Ford's company office against his representation of lesbians, who are women. Still, they must know we are ready to go with them if they ask us.

If we look at "Enough opinion believes in your own game" from MGM advertising on TV, we see a brief, efficient message about a simple fact: there are, during the presidential election, too many opinions out there; you can't choose one; it's too complicated, too confusing. You aren't smart enough. There is a simple way to resolve your quagmire. Believe in yourself, in your game and go lose your money at MGM. Whether you believe in your game or not won't change the reality that casinos exist only because they know we always eventually lose when gambling. We can always count on advertising firms to use any opportunity to exploit everything to push the interest of their clients. Even a presidential election is a good business opportunity for them.

The manipulation of the public by subliminal messaging conveyed by advertising firms is probably the most dangerous because it is constant and seemingly innocuous. It has a passive way of shoring up negative, violent, racist, sexual and vicious messages in the public mind. We see them so often that we don't notice it anymore. Neither do we notice the total absence of guilt, remorse, criticism or penalty in the messages carried by movies, plays, etc. We've been immersed, for a while now, in a in a brutal, aggressive, thuggish culture saturated by narcissists, idols, stars, moving from a cult of personality to physical vanity in a constant seamless discourse of superficiality.

And about the 'fake news' we are drowning in?

The adage 'if it bleeds it leads' is still alive in the media, but 'fake news' is in a category by itself. Our definition of it is: - "Fake news is a hoax which intends to disrupt the truth for whatever reason, by people who know the news is fake." (USDF) We are witnessing an explosion of it; it is one of the consequences of an exponential growth of the infosphere/media. From a lone wacko, in the basement of her/his parent's house, to the secret police of a foreign country they all have access to and participate in the social discourse of any country, throughout the world, without any control.

It is bad because it cripples any debate; if you get false information, you will be making fallacious arguments which will invariably result in flawed solutions. We can't blame people who vote against their own interest. Vote for what? For whom? Who is telling the truth? Well, people, we got the truth from Russian hackers about how we were bamboozled by our own DNC / Wasserman-Schultz, who shoved down our throats one Hilary. That wasn't a fake news, it was a real one and we got it from Russian hackers! That people were amazing! (They infiltrated the DNC's emails and gave them to Wikileaks.) But the media want us to forget very quickly that they double-crossed the American voters and doused us with news about the imminent danger of Russia taking over the infosphere. They, and the rest of the world, certainly use it as much as we do.

The people from megamedia are all upset now, not because of moral outrage at foreign interference in our elections, but because it wasn't them who controlled the manipulation. It is what all the shenanigans about Russian interference in the American election are all about. Don't we have enough proof that we intervene in every election, everywhere in the world? What makes us think that we will be protected from the same kind of dirty tricks, when we are the ones who put in place the NSA, which spy on the rest of the world, including the American people? A useful reminder for our readers: *"Not every item of news should be published. Rather those who control news policies must endeavor to make every item of news serve a particular purpose."* That quote from Joseph Goebbels, is true of some media outlets in America.

Our refuges? By alphabetic order, American Conservative, America, The American Interest, The Atlantic, The Cairo Review of Global Affairs, Criterion, Foreign Affairs, Lapham's, The New Yorker, Reason, Scientific American, Texas Monthly, etc. Being on that list isn't a form of endorsement from us, but a proof that there are a lot of very good magazines and journals in the US.

ARE "SNIPPETS" INNOCUOUS? NO, THEY ALSO ARE SUBLIMINAL MESSAGES!

Our eyes and ears are full of meaningless information. Let's see and give here an example with Ernie and Burt from Sesame Street, which according the 'Queer culture', are homosexual. We wish it was just a trivial little story, but when we interviewed people, we were surprised that it wasn't for them. Some families, just average American citizens told us the following. "I grew up with Bert and Ernie and was happy to share the same experience with my son and daughters. Well, I can't because those two guys are now lovers and it's not my cup of tea!" another quote, "We really don't care about the gays, but they shouldn't come into our house making my children's puppets f.....g each other." Last one "why don't homos create their own puppets and leave us alone with their obsessive sexuality" etc. (disclosure: we censured the language used by the interviewees.)

American people are upset and provoked by the culture of a minority which not only do not intend to respect their values but want them to accept, in their house, their 'Queer' culture, which is a homosexual subculture. So, when Eleanor Margolis (see newstateman.com) among others, states "some puppets are gay, get over it, Sesame Street." We don't have to "get over it" and accept children's puppets as homosexuals just to please them. It's ludicrous, children's puppets don't have a sexual life; they are just funny-looking creations to entertain children and teach them friendship, how to deal with Gros boubous, other children who don't look like them, etc. the creation of Frank OZ and Jim Henson was based on Neil Simon's 'Odd Couple' famous duo of opposite men characters. Homosexuality was never in the picture and the traditionalism is made it successful. So, when a puppeteer projects his homosexuality on the puppets, and assumes publicly, all over the media, that they are homos, well, there is something wrong.

His employer must tell him to take his homosexual militancy somewhere else than in the living room of American families.

Most people don't really care about homosexual culture as long as some people don't shove it in their throats.

We are greatly concerned by the political consequences of that minority bulldozing everywhere their way of life.

The consequences are that some families, which so far, were neutral, Democrat voters, uninvolved in the Queer world, became suspicious, hostile toward a minority which tramples their values.

People felt the contempt of a minority who basically think "F..k them!" we will do whatever we want. Well, Bernie and Bert's little story is part of a much larger reaction called populism. The fact is, the latest didn't pop out from nowhere on the US political scene but the issue is that it affected the results of 2016 election by pushing people, from our side, away from the ballot or voting for the opposite candidate *and that is our main concern, not homosexuality*! It is just one example among thousands, of 'snippets' concealed under a large variety of subjects, which are manipulating people to a level never seen before in our country. It is as dangerous as the subliminal messages of advertisements, the "fake news" etc. All that carried by the infosphere/media.

MORE ABOUT POPULISM

Populism emerged not only from the right, but as well from the left during the 2016 Presidential election. It was an emotional response by some of <u>our</u> voters, to the undemocratic, manipulative, politics of our own party. People's comprehension of their environment is based, not on some abstract cognition they don't have, but on the social and emotional perception of the consequences of an adverse politic which makes their lives worse. Their emotions are intense when they see their world collapse in front of their eyes.

American people ask themselves some basic questions like 'why is my paycheck remaining the same for several years while prices, taxes, rent increase?' Why did my parents, first generation immigrants, have a better life? Why do teachers show contempt for my boy? Why is my Asian family under so much stress? Why should I give money to educate black people when I can't even pay for my son's college tuition? Why do some people call me a racist pig when I voted twice for Obama? Why do the Europeans have a universal health care system when we don't? Why, as a young black single mother, can't my children have a good start in education? Why is my Latino daughter exposed to lesbianism in school under the cover of sexual freedom for teenagers? etc.

There is a lot of stress, emotion, and frustration going on in most social classes in America and populism is the emotional reaction to all those unanswered questions. Our group doesn't intend to blame those people, but the politically and socially incompetent, dogmatic donkeys who made it happen.

NON-PRINT MEDIA:

Hollywood/cable business is into entertaining and we get some superb and beautiful products since it is an industry and art at the same time. We must pinpoint here that it isn't Tarantino's or "Joker" type of movies which are a problem; mainly because the public pays to see it. It is under the citizens' control. We are much more concerned by shows we all receive passively during dinner when we are tired and don't pay attention. The worst is that most channels advertise the evening's coming shows by displaying the most disturbing, violent, vicious parts of it. It is a constant reiteration of short clips full of guns, explosions, pursuit, etc. every few minutes. It exerts a constant influence on all of us. Those advertising are much more dangerous than the shows themselves since they are showing violent acts out of the story's context.

We just wonder what the trustworthiness of the No Gun crowd is, when we never see them concerned by giant media exploitation of gun violence so blatantly. Probably because it is more comfortable to lament about guns than to run after Warner Brothers' psychopaths 'Suicide Squad' and Harley Quinn with her baseball bat who resolves revenge on screen for us, displaying our social problems with an absurd level of violence. Why are those people unable to face the reality of what our society is becoming and try to figure out why, and do one's best to find out where the issues are? We can put a 70 tons Abraham tank in our living-rooms, and nothing will happen to our houses, our families, our streets, our neighborhoods if human don't use it. Probably, our wood floor will suffer some serious damage.

The usual excuse from the media people is their productions reflect our social reality. We are convinced that the overwhelming diffusion of it is creating in large part that reality. They know too well that violence and sex are a sure way to make money. It has a calamitous impact on our culture. We insist we aren't calling to censure anybody. In Birth of a Nation, Nate Parker, shows the violence inherent to slavery, and there is nothing sexy about it. Will Gluck can directs Friends with Benefits, there is sex but no violence. You even can have sex and violence in the same movie, like in Woody Allen, Match Point where he made sure to disassociate both. To make violence sexy has catastrophic consequences but it is a good payoff for some. Don't we have the MPAA to protect us from that kind of abuse?

The members of it are Disney, Netflix, Paramount, Sony, Universal Warner Bros! MPAA is a trade group and don't count on it to bring a sense of moral and social responsibility to Hollywood/Cable business. We will be able to do it by bringing into the MPAA: parents' associations, educators, children's health department, etc. and give them some power. We insist on the fact that we aren't anti-business but dismayed by the irresponsibility of some business leaders.

HOW DANGEROUS ARE THE ALGORITHMS? LIKE EVERYTHING ELSE, THEY CAN BE USED FOR GOOD OR ILL

We already use them in our social life. To a great extent, they are a product of numeric science. They are only tools which can bring progress in the way to manage society's needs. The problem started, for example, when some people found it normal to use it in the justice system and work with those numbers from algorithms to decide on parole for prisoners based on their school background, zip code, medical history, family background and come up with a probability of recidivism that will affect the decision of the parole board. It is, all in all, extremely dangerous. It will effectively destroy the fundamental value of redemption, to give a human being a second chance to get her/his life back.

If we don't pay attention to how high-tech power is used, a new form of authoritarianism, based on technology, will arise via automatization of our social life based on codified information. It is the first step toward despotism, which usually ends up in totalitarianism. If someone is organizing, which means controlling, our social life, there is no need for Freedom. What will you need it for, since your freedom will be organized by people working with algorithms? *"The constant advocacy by GAFAMEDFI that those are impartial, neutral, un-biased since there is no human interfering in the inner logic of their working is a fiendish lie. There are ALWAYS humans, ordering, paying, writing, installing algorithms, ALWAYS."* (USDF) Groups of interests are placing those all over our social life.

The next step to watch for is when the finance people,

the merchants etc. will enforce on us a cashless society. As of now some corporations already have, at the retail level, stores which refuse cash. With all due respect to merchants, we can't accept being tricked the same way GAFA did. We must not accept cashless businesses. It is the last step for establishing a police regime in the US worse than communism. "Not only the finance people, Banks, FBI, NSA, CIA, Government, ONGs, hackers etc. will know 24/7/365 ALL OUR MOVES, all the time, ABSOLUTELY nothing will escape their surveillance of the American people as we will have an electronic mark-up on all our moves." (USDF) If they succeed, we will be living in something call Capitalo-communism, somehow the flip side of the Chinese communist state-capitalism. Here, we want to give a big thank you to Richie Torres, Raphael Espinal, Corey Jonhson, who fought and helped pass in New York a rule making cashless businesses illegal since 12% of people living in New York don't use a bank.

SUPERCONGLOS OWN THE INFOSPHERE/ MEDIA TO SERVE THEIR INTERESTS

We don't think AT&T, a telecommunication giant co., a resurrected Mabel after a multitude of convolutions, paid $85 billion for Time/Warner to be nice with us! That corporation's debt is now around $180 billion. They want to gain back their investment and don't want anybody to rock the boat. They need a very passive population, who will ingurgitate as much as possible: goods, entertainment, funny politic etc. The last thing they want is to have an efficient press around, an educated citizenry who could ask too many questions about what exactly they are doing.

The infosphere is first a tool and we must learn how to use it, starting in school. If we make the effort to look for material written by the well informed, we can find it everywhere: in a library, in a good bookstore, on the Internet, on TV, anywhere. We just need to find how to learn to separate the wheat from the chaff. Nobody from GAFAMEDFI will offer a valuable and truthful piece on Saudi Arabia that explains what has happened to that country. A half a century ago it was a decent place to live by Middle Eastern standards. Information from the infosphere will not trace and give us the why for its deterioration. Information is available but it is like a game of Where's Waldo?

How can we fix that problem? We must learn how to connect the dots, to bridge the significant facts to each other. We have the right to receive clear and coherent information; it is a requirement of democracy. It isn't a fundamental right of MegaCorps to give us the news they want to give us. It's called proselytism, indoctrination, propaganda when they do.

We have laws in our political arsenal to fight Conglomeration. Let's use it to dismantle the news cartels. Expect a huge fight, with them screaming bloody murder. Of course, they will resort to 'freedom of the press'! Which is in fact 'don't touch our freedom to use our press'. We must fight for our right to real information.

THIS IS WHAT YOU CAN DO WHEN YOU OWN THE MEDIA

Here we need to quote Marshall McLuhan: "Today the tyrant rules not by club or fist, but disguised as a market researcher, he shepherds his flock in the way of utility and comfort." Sometimes they do believe in what they write and say. If not, they can be bought quite easily. If they don't follow the rules of the group's interests, they will end up working somewhere else or unemployed. The controlling interests of the media do not let anything escape their watchful eyes. The Big Six own or control now 90% of all media but it's concealed under hundreds and hundreds of subsidiaries which hide that concentration of power from the public. The infosphere is not under the brute force of censure. It is a much more insidious, sophisticated way to control the content of the social discourse. They use silence. They never bring up to the front page the real issues. You must fill out the silence or people are going to notice something is wrong. It is where the entertainment business and the useful idiots are so handy.

We certainly have fine articles written about the deindustrialization in specialized magazines, but rarely when they should, do they reach the front page of major newspapers or prime time TV. Instead we notice the media publishing glowing reviews of a book by a distinguished male feminist professor from SUNY, Stony Brook. His book *Angry White Men* argues that they should stop whining when they lose their jobs and positions of power, which was to drive a truck, assemble cars, build airplanes for a paycheck. He was too busy to chastise them and their entitlement; and couldn't see, in Michigan, the impact of the deindustrialization which ruined, not only white, but all minority working men and their families, their communities, their cities, their states. Instead he published a Guys' Guide to feminism because feminism is good for men. Well, BadFeminism which controls it, is so good that he was himself accused, anonymously, by a woman, of 'unethical conduct'. Did it shatter a few of his male feminist convictions? We don't know and don't care. We prefer to care for the consequences of deindustrialization.

LET'S SUMMARIZE THIS CHAPTER

It is critical that we get information from varied sources. Contrasting viewpoints can help us understand an issue by giving us other perspectives on the same fact base.

Who doesn't remember how the war in Iraq was sold to the citizenry with a shamefully dishonest big media using propaganda that would be familiar in an autocracy? It is easy for us to recall the: "We need that war to save peace in the Middle East!" Really? It cost $3 ½ trillion to the American taxpayers, and certainly bought no peace in the Middle East to speak of.

We were conned by the media that ignored the incompetence of the Bush administration who had people confused between Nigeria and Niger and about "yellow cake" bought by Saddam Hussein to build his nuclear weapons. Who can forget the character assassination of Joseph Wilson who, after returning from Africa, reported that none of it was true? Should we mention breaking the cover of his wife, Valerie Plame, a clandestine CIA agent?

Of course, so-called information used by the media were from "people not authorized to speak publicly," or from shady operatives of dubious reliability, like an Italian spy who got first class information from a mysterious informant from a very small country in the Middle East.

And in 2017, we had to swallow the "Dossier Christopher Steele," which was just a sulfurous bag of trash which, and that is unbelievable, the FBI thought was credible. It is what started the investigation on Donald Trump's campaign. It is amazing that people like James B. Comey, Director of the FBI, a Republican, let it happen. Oops sorry, we need to stop here. We said that our only concern is our side. So, our question is why the Democrat party lost two precious years, doing a rain dance, hoping we would get a miraculous impeachment from the Mueller report, instead of laying the foundation of a real political program showing our capacity to govern as opposed to just undoing Donald Trump's politic.

We are just fed up, tired of the ineptitude of our political leaders. It cost us our dignity, our integrity, and nothing, absolutely nothing had been resolved politically in the Middle East or in our country. The role of the media was of primordial importance in both fiascos!

But rejoice, people! We still can again call our snacks 'French fries' and not 'Liberty Fries'. -the French never call their fries French anyway. They are from Belgium.

We just hope that A.G. Sulzberger and his colleagues understand that it isn't Donald Trump who destroyed the credibility of the press and the Infosphere they did, and do it all by themselves every day, by spreading truncated, manipulated news, which ended up 'fake', by shamelessly choosing to support any kind of ideological pet project from the great grand bazaar of ideas from society's most awful. The president's tweets? It should be their last preoccupation!

NOTES

1. Elizabeth Kolbert, who owns the Internet? What Big Tech's monopoly powers mean for our culture, New Yorker, Aug.28, 2017

2. We can summarize it to: She was a young woman in her twenties, who left Los Angeles telling her friends she took her knee pads with her, just in case; and during her internship in the White House, gave, willingly oral sex to the President

3. Even people with the best intentions are hoodwinked by the media: Figures behind child prostitutes overinflated? New York newspaper questions number used in Ashton Kutcher – Demi Moore ad campaign, "real men don't buy girl", nbcnews.com, 06-29-2011. We are not criticizing those two actors who believe in the source of information which is manipulating them.

4. The equivalent will be to have Hilary Clinton being president and "madam Irma" giving her advice on how to run the country, and both of them making money from it.

5. See a book written by Jodi Kantor and Megan Twobey. She said, "We highly recommend it since the authors dig deep enough to show the collusion between some 'feminist lawyers' cashing out millions on settlements instead of stopping the aggression by sending the rapist to court where they would have gotten less money"

6. The famous adapted quote from Friedrich Nietzsche, "there are no facts but an interpretation," was found in one of his notebooks. It has never been a fully developed theory, but the post modernists use it to death in the debate between realists and anti-realists. Our daily language is so full of manipulation. What used to be a used car is now a 'pre-owned car', ignorance is 'strength',' war is for peace', a sales clerk is an 'associate', etc.

MISCELLANY

1. Media giants: who own what, www.edul.edu
2. The word algorithm derives from algorithmic, which was the Latinization of Mohammad-in-Musa-alkwarizmi, Persian scholar in mathematics and astronomy.
3. When you buy a book written by Herman Melville it doesn't mean that you "like" or "don't like" it, but that you want to read it.
4. "My heart was light and joyful in my work, because the decisions weren't mine". Alan Rosenthal, Eichmann Revisited, The Jerusalem Post, 20 April 2011. That way of thinking is familiar with all people working for large organizations and they don't have to be fascist murderers but can become.
5. Quote from an angry interviewee, 29-year-old professional man. 'We noticed, during our informal research, that a lot, we mean a lot, of American people are really angry! It is our responsibility to know why and act accordingly.'
6. This is an example of what people call being an offensive academic "fake ass".
7. The 2018 shooting at Parkland School in Florida was done by someone who didn't own a gun and was able to buy one because of a clerical mistake from the FBI. Someone forgot to put the murderer's name on the alert list that all gun sellers must consult before selling one. 2012 Sandy Hook massacre was done by somebody who shot his sleeping mother in the face and went on to kill 20 children between 6 and 7 years old, total casualty 26 people. Misogyny has absolutely nothing to do with it. An administrative snafu and mental illness are the explanations.

SUPERCONGLOS

DISCLOSURE: IF OUR group had a much better economic system to offer, our readers would be the first ones
to be informed. In between, we certainly can improve,
upgrade the one we have, and put it back on the right
track. But SuperConglos doesn't intend to let it happen
since it is contradictory to their interests.

"History suggests that capitalism is a necessary
condition for political freedom. Clearly it is not a
sufficient condition." Milton Friedman

"In the Soviet Union, capitalism triumphed over
communism. In this country capitalism triumphed over democracy." Fran Leibovitz

"The United States is not a nation to which peace
is a necessity." Grover Cleveland.

"The Infosphere/media complex is in essence the
'nerve gas' of the ruling interests of our country."
(USDF)

MEGACORPS AND INFOSPHERE

We saw that they basically control the infosphere/ media complex. They don't need to own all newspapers, TV stations, movie studios, and publishing companies; they just need to have a controlling interest in them to use it to their advantage. But how did we arrive in this situation?

It started under the Republican Ronald Reagan presidency but reached an absurd level with a piece of legislation, the Digital Media Act, signed by Bill Clinton a Democrat president on October 28, 1996. "The most anti-democratic piece of legislation, passed in the 20th century" according to media scholar, Bob McChesney. President Clinton said, "We will support removal of judicial and legislative restrictions on all types of telecommunications companies: cable, telephone, utilities, television and satellites. Market forces replace regulations and judicial models that are no longer appropriate." [1]

As Michael Moore says: "Bill Clinton was a pretty good president for a Republican." Ah, the wonder of deregulation when it is done by the Democrats; unfortunately, it was the wrong kind! We are living with its consequences. Now we have five media super-mega-conglomerates that have absorbed everything they could get their hands on. Together they tacitly say: To Hell with that democracy! We can make as much money without it, look at our billionaire Chinese friends and their authoritarian/state capitalism. We just need to control the state and it will be done. From the evolution of a liberal economic system emerged that neo-liberalism which buttresses supercorps. Well, those are having a dramatic effect on our lives. We saw in the previous chapter that those who control the media, have an incredibly powerful way to dominate the social discourse.

We are dealing with an aggregation of conglomerates, where disputes, brutal conflicts, disagreements are numerous, but where the market economy is under the sway of those economic giants. The last step for the latest is to have political power. They want it because they need to bring into being their undemocratic rules based on their economic interests only.

Let's go back to AT&T, that communication-technology giant. It was barely in the entertainment business; but still bought Time Warner for $ 80 billion (total debt of that corporation is now $180 billion). Some people think a lot of synergy exists between both businesses. Not really, but AT&T wanted to be an active partner in controlling a slice of the social discourse because they know the importance of it. MegaCorps are heavily involved in grabbing the attention of people which must be diverted toward everything peripheral to the foundational principles of society, owing to the fact that *'Attention' isn't 'Information.'* The latest is a different step which can be circumvented if you keep the attention 'on' 24/7/365. (see ADDENDUM)

Entertainment, from superb to silly, is a great way to do it and it can be loaded with any content you want. But it also creates a kind of numbness among the population and it is a sight to behold since people can be distracted ad infinitum, especially if you add dope, alcohol, happy pills, gambling etc. The deep consequences of living that way is the stupefying effect of that culture which makes American people less intelligent than 30 years ago. It's very difficult now for anyone to think rationally, intelligently, since the tools to do it have disappeared from our education and general culture.

The night shows are funny, thanks to the sharp writing and talent of artists involved. But notice that all TV channels have the same kinds of programs. We want to focus on the ones that poke fun at our politics and politicians. But to make fun of the president's haircut doesn't make anybody understand the impact of the new tax code. People think that television which ridicules absurdities in our political life offers real insight into political problems. Nothing is further from the truth. Satire does not bring any insight; it just offers enjoyment and an opportunity for viewers to vent their own personal frustrations. *"Most people don't realize that progressively 'infotainment' has morphed into 'politainment', aka, politics as entertainment."* (USDF) As a consequence, Jon Stewart became the anti-Walter Cronkite of the news business.

A FEW FACTS TO PUT OUR DISCUSSION IN PERSPECTIVE

Capitalism is one of many economic systems and we must be unequivocal in letting our readers realize that we make a fundamental distinction between capitalism and its perversion called economic oligarchy, MegaCorps, SuperConglos, etc. Capitalism has undeniable qualities (it isn't a 'lip service' when we write it), like entrepreneurship, risk-taking, competition which are indispensable to any modern society etc. It is at its best when it works in a democratic context where the rules aren't crooked, contorted, bent to favor, for example, SuperCapital.

Our market economy did not begin with capitalism. Exchange between people can be traced from the beginning of time. The Phoenicians traded with Africans 2300 B.C., Leonardo Fibonacci, aware of the financial needs of trading, applied the Indo-Arabic numeral mathematical concept to exchange in 1202 A.D. It was enormous progress in the management of trade to produce a plus value of consequences. It was the money from trade which financed the industrialization of the Western world. From it, rolled in modern capitalism, with its sophisticated financial system. So, capitalism as we know it, the combination of industry and finance, is a relatively recent outcome of the evolution of the economic world. [2]

We shouldn't be frightened by MegaCorps, even if their power is awesome.

But in this chapter, we, simply, try to save Supercapitalism from itself; because it is making a huge mistake by attacking democracy – the backbone of its success. It is our responsibility to remind people in charge, that they are the ones who increased economic inequality which has accelerated since the 1970s. 75% of the general population got poorer even when unemployment went down. We aren't happy about it.

THE SUPER-MANAGERS

First, let's look at economic inequality's most flagrant outrage: The super manager's salary. With the help of the media we now have the 'celebrated CEO'. They certainly deserve a good salary but not at the obscene levels that we now have. Some CEOs are earning over $120 million per year! $10 million a month! $2,141,857.14 a week, $305,979 a day, plus perks like private jets, limos, etc. It's sickening. We are the only country in the world that pays these salaries to a manager. These millions should go to investors and workers, from a decent CEO to the janitor. We must put a brake on this level of greed. Too many big cheeses have their compensation bound to stock prices, so to push the stock's price up they make more money, sometimes to the detriment of the corporation.

If there are some corporations too big to fail, there aren't boards of directors, CEOS, CFOs etc. who aren't too big to fail. We shouldn't hesitate to give them a good push without a golden parachute. Let's remember that when the 'S&L' scandal happened, President Reagan's government put around 1,000 people in jail. In 2008, when the financial crack occurred, not one person went to jail; from financial scandal to financial crack, we expunged the concept of responsibility in the financial world. Something must change in the way we handle white-collar criminality. In Japan, Carlos Ghosn, CEO of Renault-Nissan-Mitsubishi: one of the biggest automakers in the world, is in jail for tax reasons, it is that simple! In two generations, our government went from criminal prosecution to collecting fines, like SuperConglos care about them!

THE POLITICAL POWER OF BIG BUSINESS

J.P. Morgan, Henry Ford, Rothschild, Rockefeller or Carnegie, were as powerful as Eli Broad, Larry Page, Bill Gates, Sergey Brin or Jeff Bezos. Teddy Roosevelt, Justice Louis Brandeis stared them down and were successful. [3]

Aware of the dangers to democracy presented by the super powerful corporations, the Sherman Anti-Trust Act was passed in 1880. The government started using it to defend its citizens against runaway avarice of big business. The New Haven Railroad, controlled by J.P. Morgan, was one of their targets. The government was successful at making sure it didn't become a monopoly. When it happened J.P. Morgan screamed bloody murder and hated trustbuster, Teddy Roosevelt, for the rest of his life. Morgan's financial status was not significantly affected, but his political clout was. It is what we are after, good business must back off from politics. MegaConglos went much, much too far; we understand very well that business must have a voice but not to the extent of taking over the country!

Let's take another example of a successful dismantling of a giant corporation: Ma Bell. In 1984, Bell Telephone had one million employees and $150 billion in business. It was bigger than G.M., IBM, US Steel, and Eastman Kodak combined! After the monopoly was dismantled, there were many unhappy customers who saw their phone bills increase by as much as 40%. But long-distance calls went down 38% and, most important of all, the end of the monopoly created a vital space for all the start-up extraordinary technological innovation. Most of today's high-tech success resulted from the breakup of this monopoly. People at the time thought they had killed a nefarious dragon, but in fact they killed a big cow. Ma Bell was the de facto ministry of telecommunications for the US government.

If capitalism, as engine of innovation in our society, is smothered out by super-capital, we should just get rid of super-capitalism which lost its justification as a creative force for our society. They certainly are a creative force for themselves, but they turn it against us (deindustrialization) when their interests are at stake. Still, we must write that economic concentration is a key phase in the development of capital. It isn't bad in itself; it is a logical step in the evolution of the world economic model. But the problems become evident when it mutates into conglomerations which want political power. We are facing it since the size of their business is so large that it can ignore the needs, the will, of any human society, including ours. They will follow several steps to reach that goal.

The first one is to cut the money supply to the government by not paying taxes. Thus, it won't be able to face its responsibility and all public services will collapse. Supercorps will come in and offer to take charge of it since the government is not able to face its responsibility. Social security, education, retirement, Medicare/Medicaid, DMW etc. will be privatized for the greatest benefit of some MegaCorps, which will create an autarchic economic-politic system in control globally of our society. Democracy will be dead. We simplify but it is not a simplistic way to look at it.

SUPERCAPITAL DOESN'T LIKE NATION-STATE

According to the mathematical equation r. > g., in Thomas Piketty's book [4], economic revenue is bigger than economic growth. It answers the question of how and why some get richer while the masses get poorer. If the economy, (i.e., goods production) is booming, money can trickle down to a lower economic rung. But when wealth is created outside of a country nothing, or very little, trickles down. Some consider Piketty's theory unsustainable. However, this belief appears to be false given the consistent economic inequality that capitalism seems to create.

Western capitalism was born out of a marriage between traditional liberalism, democracy, Enlightenment and republicanism, without which it would not have survived. There have been many magnificent civilizations in world history: the Inca, the Muslim Arabs, the Chinese, India and others. They were superior to anything that existed in Europe in that time. When people in London were living in huts, 1,000. B.C. Alexandria, in Egypt, had an average of 300,000 papyrus collections in its library; they also had streetlights at night, based on oil, etc.

Yet, they were all left in the dust by the European Enlightenment. Without it, modern capitalism would not have emerged from the Dark Middle Ages. The nation-state, democracy and capitalism were a ménage-a-trois forming the bedrock of Western civilization. Super finance capital, filled with money, power and arrogance now thinks it doesn't need anybody anymore. It wants the freedom to operate as it pleases but to maintain itself, it must remove democracy/liberalism, values/norm and nation-states systems which historically maintained a balance between the needs and obligations of its social forces.

We are witnessing a total change in our economic system. That reversal has its consequences: it makes us live in something else. Is that something else a thing that we really want?

HOW FAR CAN THEY GO TO WEAKEN IT?

The goal of the MegaCorps isn't to destroy the nation state, but to weaken it to such an extent that it stands only to collect taxes to pay for the lucrative contracts the new oligarchy got from the government. If there are taxes to pay, somebody needs to provide loopholes. A weak state under their control, with a very strong army, would be perfect. They would be able to do business the way they want without the inconvenient encumbrance of laws, regulations etc. *"This is what we have to face now: SuperConglos is in the process of neutering the State and replacing it by what they spent their time trying to convince us, the efficiency of conglomerate management."* (USDF) Naturally, owning the infosphere/media complex is a big help to propagate such a fairy tale. So SuperConglos' efficiency is for what exactly? Is it simply for them to get more powerful, richer? What else, since we don't have a clue of where we are going as a nation? (see ADDENDUM)

Let's illustrate what we mean: a response to the Great Depression was the passage in 1933 of the Glass-Steagall Act, separating investment banks from deposit banks. The law stood until it was repealed, after intensive lobbying by the bank industry. President Bill Clinton signed the Gramm-Leach-Billey Act in 1999. He wanted to adapt and improve the Glass-Steagall Act to fit the needs of a modern economy. Nothing wrong with that. But, unfortunately, critical safeguards were removed and never replaced. Obviously, the bankers didn't intend to replace Glass-Steagall, because regulations place limitations on their freedom to do business the way they want.

President Clinton's silence created a vacuum in which investment banks rushed in, using massive sums of money to play with! With so much cash from the American public deposit on hand, the loan business was booming. The Republicans didn't see anything wrong with President George Bush's position that "every American should own their home." It was full of good intentions. Well, eight years down the road, kaboom! Millions and millions of American people were ruined and lost their homes which, for most, was their largest asset.

Let's recap., a Democrat president (Clinton), by removing the safety roadblocks of sound banking, set up the housing crisis. A Republican president (G. Bush) didn't see anything wrong since business was booming. Then another Democrat president (Barak Obama) bailed out those responsible for it because he didn't believe he had a choice. In other words, the way to Hell is paved with good intentions, but it didn't stop some people from cashing out big time on it. Naturally, again we had to reduce to essentials a very sophisticated system of power/control but when you streamline everything this is where it ends up.

So, to weaken a nation-state: ask people you elected to remove the laws that are obstacles to your interests. It's that simple. The social and human cost doesn't matter since they call it progress. Books and books were written on the negative effect of these economics. We don't need to write one more. We just want to alert people about their retirement plans.

Are they safe in the hands of the private capital? A California pension plan, calPERS, lost $½ billion with BlackRock. Some studies suggest a $4 trillion deficit in our retirement plans. Police, teachers, fire departments all over the country are in precarious positions. They are mostly managed by private funds that are risking money in the markets. [5]

We certainly can use extensive amounts of our money for the development of our country. However, we must do a much better job at controlling our funds and protecting our retirement funds. We don't have any confidence in the people who didn't see or do anything to stop the collapse of 2008.

The 2008 economic crisis posed a crisis for whom? Not Citibank? Bank of America? They got bigger and more powerful! We can predict another crisis since we will be obliged to bail the 'too big to fail' again. Did our party come up with some creative solution to resolve that problem? No, it didn't; it's just waiting for the next crisis which will require urgent solutions to save the day, and those solutions never go through the normal democratic processes. It shouldn't, considering that an economic crisis is good, on the long term, for business. It shattered all businesses which are an impediment to economic concentration; it is called 'creative destruction'. It is the favorite tool used by neo-liberals to advance their interests. That version of economic-neo-liberalism is the perfect instrument to put into place a system of 'permanent crisis'. (see ADEDDENDUM)

To illustrate our argument, let's look at some numbers. On September 25th, 2008, the FDIC took over Washington Mutual and sold it the next day to J.P. Morgan/Chase for $1.9 billion. The assets of WaMu included $307 billion! Chase, which didn't want any money from the $700 billion Tarp, but was obliged, (it's not a joke) by our government to take around $14 billion. Chase certainly didn't need the money to pay for that superb deal.

Was Jamie Dimon brilliant in the way he steered his bank through those troubled times? He certainly was, but you see that isn't the point. The point is, our elected government used our public money, to bail banks out because it didn't have any other option. No reason for us to criticize President Obama on his decision. But we are facing a mutation of capitalism itself into something radically different. The rationale justifying capitalism is gone and is replaced by MegaCorps'. *"Public finance assuming risk taken by private capital is a total reversal of the power dynamic in the country, and we must face the reality of it. Capitalism used to be the economic expression of democracy. Now democracy is the political expression of super-capitalism!"* (USDF) Do we want people responsible for that switch in charge of our retirement funds? Well, in fact, it's just a subsidiary question, the real one is, do we want those people in charge of our country? Because their goal is to take over the presidency and privatize Social Security, Medicare, education etc. [6] There is no more pretense on their part.

We are saying that we must protect ourselves from those economic interests. We must shove decency and morality down some throats, or we and our children are going to have a very painful wake-up call. The alarm is on; don't push the snooze button, please.

We ought to create safeguards providing strong protective structures. The ones existing are too weak or corrupted by the existing system. *"Legally we could create a 'Public Trust' to protect basic public service like health care, education, Social Security, Medicare and secure it with an amendment to the Constitution."* USDF We are in favor of improving all public management systems and use private initiative know how, we aren't fan of big Government, but we must never let the private sector be in charge of it alone.

IMPORTANCE OF CULTURES AND MORAL/VALUES IN THE BUSINESS WORLD

The "everything which is not illegal is legal" attitude, the complacency of high finance and MegaCorps laissez faire, at any cost, must stop!

We don't need to demonize anybody; but the leadership of GAFA is out of control. They've lost all social and historical perspective. They are adrift in their newness, thinking that the latest high-tech gizmo is going to save the day. Hedge funds, banks are all playing a game of who is going to invent the most perplexing, opaque, sophisticated, arcane accounting system that nobody can understand. They don't want anybody else to understand what they are doing. They all live in their own created "alternate reality" disassociated from the rest of us. We aren't talking about the local or the state banks, we are talking about super, megafinance.

Their business reaches around the globe, and encompasses many disparate cultures based on extremely different values. The best solution is for them to flatten all cultures and make the planet one large unified market. To reach that goal they must coerce all nations to adopt a solidified neo-liberal-economic legal system to make the market work in conformity worldwide. But those laws are affecting deeply all national cultures which reflect the history of humankind and you can't disregard it that easily. Because all cultures fuse, coalesce with *human beings' identity*. It is where their problem is. Hard core MegaCorps neo-liberals won't be satisfied until they modify the comportment, meaning to alter what a human being is. *"Chiefly, they think we aren't docile enough to swallow all the goods they want us to buy and that we show too often an aversion for the outcome of their neo-liberalism"* (USDF). They count first on that modern arsenal of tools called infosphere/media to reach their goals, which is to turn our freedom into voluntary servitude. If they can't succeed, the stick will come later.

They certainly are masters at creating and moving goods, but their knowledge of humanity comes from their marketing department which is certainly sophisticated! But they are fooling themselves if they think they have dominion or will have jurisdiction over humans. They aren't the first ones trying.

They can bamboozle us to some tragic extent, but somehow human nature is extremely resilient. We spend our time taking three steps forward and two backward, but at the end we can extract ourselves from the worst. This is where our hopes rest. The neo-liberals shouldn't forget that someone in Beirut can wear Nike shoes, Lewis jeans, Cardi B's T. and slash their throat humming the latest from Taylor Swift. "Unifying all markets to sell goods doesn't change anything in human socio-political reality. *"Their basic social motto is 'money talks, bullshit walks!'; well, it is time for them to 'talk the talk' and justify their existence by being something else than gigantic money vacuum cleaners!"* (USDF) (see ADDENDUM)

SUPER-CAPITALISTS COULD BUY OR BORROW A SENSE OF MORALITY

Most of the capitalists are individually charitable, but that does not translate into a sense of morality in business. In fact, they give away money to help make that issue disappear. They don't have to think about it anymore while focusing on their corporation making billions at any social cost.

It is not reasonable to expect corporations to have a sense of morals on their own, it is not their priority. As Milton Friedman said, "The social responsibility of business is to increase profits. That's all."

We don't have any problem with such a statement. Consequently, morality must come to these people from outside. Max Weber, in *The Protestant Ethic and the Spirit of Capitalism*, gives us an example of how this works. It was Protestant religious values, coupled with the secular values of republicanism which helped capitalism to develop into what it is now. It morphed into an intermediary period called progressivism which ended with Bill Clinton's period. Now we are in the MegaCorps period.

Branko Milanovic gives us an excellent perspective on how SuperConglos can resolve their morality deficit, calling it "outsourcing morality." We must re-establish a basic set of moral values in business and use laws to make the business world respect them. The three institutional branches of our government must agree on using a big stick if necessary to implement them. We can forecast a brutal and fierce backlash from GAFAMEDFI complex which will fight tooth and nail against any proposal that limits their power. It's an old story, but we can't and won't let some people with power make us live in a society without social values—only economic ones.

We do not want a rehash of the good old days when a homosexual had to hang himself in his closet, because socially he couldn't be accepted, when a woman's world was limited to her house, when a Black couldn't have a shot at success, when the life of a White miner was so cheap that Virginia's coal mines didn't bother to let local newspapers know he died in the mine, etc. It was the sense of justice from our values which made progressively the society, composed of everybody, a more decent place to live. Social values are never 'old', they evolve. We replaced an 18th century concept of honor (people killing each other in duels over some perceived slight), with 'see you in court'.

Now, some call for new moral standards based on greed, narcissism, dogmatism, racism, sexualism, violence which are now ubiquitous, permanent in our daily lives, and common economic practices. We don't have any confidence in the business elites who will behave with only a logic from economy and not a logic inherent to social values which, in fact, aren't conflicting. A prosperous America is really very good for business. What counts are the humans and they understand well that private enterprise, fair and judicious taxes, a competent government, which does not interfere in the private lives of its citizens, are the way to go.

IS THE LEADERSHIP OF MEGACORPS IN FAVOR OF DEMOCRACY?

Some of us on the Left have made the mistake of believing the capacity of the Neo-Liberalism movement to absorb and digest any and every kind of controversy, thinking that this was proof of the ideological tolerance of that economic system. That proof was based upon a false assumption.

In truth, *"the Neo-Liberalism movement has the ability to absorb the random plethora of differing ideas because it has become ideologically empty. It now exists without a social core value system - it is for all intents and purposes, a void."* (USDF) Because of this, it is willing and able to be filled with anything.

There seems to be no idea or trend in the Neo-Liberalism movement, which is rejected, except those that are purely economic. So, there is plenty of room for the incompetents and their recklessness to fill that void. The useful idiots are just the cache-sex of Neo-Liberalism.

A lot of our Super-CEOs fancy themselves as a sort of 'John Galt' (Ayn Rand, in *Atlas Shrugged*), who see their work constantly under attack by weak parasites like you and us.

From their high perch, they wag their fingers at us about our voting habits! The arrogance of these people is limitless. For example, we have Apple CEO, Tim Cook, who fought courageously the government intent to use GAFA to spy on the citizen but interferes in state law regarding what he considers discrimination against homosexuals.

It happens that we also disagree with the way that state laws were written, but there are several problems with Mr. Cook's approach: Apple doesn't belong to him alone, even if he is a major stockholder. *"When someone is using a corporate pulpit, to advocate the private and personal matter of a CEO and to use the power of that corporation to rescind a popular vote by citizens of a state, a line was crossed, and it is not acceptable."* (USDF) for a CEO to think it is a normal procedure to do away with universal suffrage. It is time for us to make that kind of CEOS understand they must back off.

The right to vote is the guarantee of our freedom. All corporate heads should "mind their own business" because now we see too many of them every day in the media, showing us how responsible they are! Starbucks closed their stores nationwide for several hours to promote a ridiculous campaign to show that Howard Schultz is serious about racial discrimination, when disciplining one employee would have been enough. But making such an ostentatious show was just what Mr. Schultz wanted. He was plastered all over the media promoting Starbuck's social responsibility, making sure we all understood he was the progressive mind behind it.[8] Naturally, in any bookstore we have *The Ride of a Lifetime: Lessons learned from 15 years as CEO of the Walt Disney company,"* by Robert Iger. You also can find Mr. Benioff's, *Trailblazer, the Power of Business as the Greatest Platform for Change.* We don't want to forget Stephen Schwarzman, Chairman/CEO of Blackstone: *What It Takes: Lessons in the Pursuit of Excellence.* Those people certainly think they are ready to be in charge of a MegaCorp's presidency.

Marc Benioff, CEO of Salesforce, went on 60 Minutes to brag about his commitment to gender equality in his salaried work force. The total cost to the company was a paltry $3 million per year, over 8.39 billion revenue in 2017. Six percent of his employees required a salary adjustment and "roughly the same number of women and men were impacted." Meaning that 3% of women were paid less than their male colleagues, and 3% of men were paid less than their women colleagues!

We must congratulate Mr. Benioff [9] for his shrewdness in getting hundreds of millions of dollars worth of free publicity by sucking that poor dead dry horse of salary discrepancy on '60 Minutes.' Lesley Stahl didn't want to go into detail because that would have contradicted the official bamboozle that women are grossly underpaid. But why didn't Jeff Fager, executive producer of 60 Minutes, see that crude manipulation by the journalist, since she was careful to never ask the right questions. The lies continue. It's us, the tele-spectators, who had to do some research to give our readers the real picture on that issue. Steve Kraft in the next two segments of the same show, gave us detailed, well-explained facts on the dangerous practice of a discount airline which put the safety of its clients at risk by cutting corners on the maintenance of their airplanes. So, the manipulation of the public concerns only some specific matter which is essential to the dominant ideological discourse. Does Lesley Stahl believe that women are grossly underpaid? It doesn't matter but we know she is paid to say so.[10]

Plenty of CEOs see themselves now as some moral and social authorities over the citizenry. Lloyd Blankfein, chairman of Goldman Sachs, is a patron of 'LGBTQ+++'. About the presumptuous Nike's Mark Parker, who takes a stand against the flag and the National Anthem by supporting Colin Kaepernick's kneeling. They both don't get the fact that the relevance of those symbols is nonsensical since we have so many other ways to express our political disagreement. How about bringing a 25' long 4' high banner with your message on it? If you want to be into politics, be smart--don't offend people who want to help you.

We also have the pedantic Mr. Kitts, Gillette's CEO, who wants to teach American men how to be real men when shaving. We certainly can't forget Adam Neumann, who used to impose on his employee's vegetarianism, by removing from the company's cafeteria any food that was not following his diet. If some employees eat outside, they won't get reimbursed, if they don't follow the vegetarian diet of their boss! That kind of political advocacy is thoroughly self-serving. Basically, they will sell any values, any human right to make a buck or to fulfill any of their indulgences.

As we write above, we must fight back all those bloated, turgid CEOS. We can create a non-partisanship group, reaching people from both sides of the aisle. Agree on a specific goal to target the most obnoxious one.

THEY DON'T INTEND TO STOP HALFWAY

But it is not only narcissism; it is a political strategy quite well thought out. Lawrence Fink, CEO of Blackrock, which is the largest investor in the world--managing between $7 to 8 trillion in 401k plans, portfolios, equities, mutual funds, etc. sent a letter to the head of all corporations in which Blackrock has financial interest. It informed them that they must now do more than just make profits to maintain Blackrock's support; they also must contribute to society in a tangible way. In his words, "To prosper over time, every company must not only deliver financial performance, but also exhibit how it makes a positive contribution to the society." He intends to "hold companies accountable" and is already hiring people to monitor them. Accountable to whom? For what? He proclaims that too many governments are failing to prepare for the future on issues ranging from retirement and infrastructure to automation and worker training.

What he is failing to say is that administrations at every level, national and local, are all strapped for cash in large part because a shocking number of corporations, especially outsized ones, pay little or no taxes. Thus, states, cities, counties are unable to fulfill their responsibilities toward the citizenry.

The impact of this? States resort to legalizing marijuana, gambling both online and in casinos, cut basic services like Medicaid, food stamps, subway maintenance etc. to balance their budgets. But is this the correct response to financial problems?

(California cities begin embracing cannabis in desperate search for cash, Mr. Alexander Nieves wrote in 2006 (politico.com, 06-20-06.)

These solutions create even more and bigger problems. Drug addiction, black market, prostitution, gambling, gangsterism, emergence of an unstable, underclass are all side effects and are draining state's financial coffers even more. We noticed the silence of Eric Dyson and his friends who are so vocal on the sins of America but are a total no-show regarding these transgressions. Even a billionaire like Mike Bloomberg said that legalizing marijuana is even stupider than prohibition.

Too many people on our left side don't want to see the

consequences of legalizing pot smoking. We are in favor of the medical use of it, with urine tests to stop abuses. The pot heads should get a fine when caught with three ounces of grass; in case of recidivism, put on hours of community service, cleaning up bedpans of drug users with brains destroyed by bad trips. If you drive and kill people when under influence of any kind of drug or alcohol, or stockpile several tons of it in your basement, well, a long jail sentence must be applied. If you expose your children to secondhand smoke, they could end up in foster care, because your carelessness will affect the child's brain development! Do we need to wait ten years to see the consequences of drug use? Don't we have enough examples of it right now in our daily lives?

We shouldn't forget that when we will be revolted, disgusted, horrified by what's going on in our country, we will always have the 'freedom' to go to the store next door, and weed away our sense of revolt, social responsibility, and our citizen dignity. Marijuana is already four to five times more potent, and addictive, than the one from the sixties.

Is the fight from drug addiction included in the positive contributions that corporations must make to pass the 'Lawrence Fink test' of good behavior? Or does he and his small group of people try to twist the arms of other corporations to jump on the band wagon of their political ambitions? Those MegaCorps want to convince us that they are a credible alternative to a duly elected government. Why are we more than suspicious of such a claim?

Because they didn't wait. They already impose their rules on us and act like they oversee our country.

Citigroup's Barbara J. Desoer, takes a position against lines of credit for gun factories. The removal of cash money for transactions by the likes of Amazon to financial institutions, under economic efficiency, are all highly political decisions. Those are the responsibility of the Congress, Senate, elected people, not from self-appointed businesspeople. Because "Those guys aren't into social activism as they pretend, they are into political activism" (USDF).

We would like our readers to remember all the hoopla from major conglomerates which wanted to breastfeed us with their corporate culture. They already tried, in the '80s, to push their employees very hard to switch their values to the corporate one, considering that they 'took care' of us by giving a salary. So, their logic is 'you depend on us so you must adopt our values', which most working people in America answered, justly, by a loud GFY given that without us they would be nothing! It's funny how those people always forget that without a work force their beautiful creations would be just a pipe dream! So, since they failed to impose their ideas on us at the corporate level they moved to the step above, in sync with conglomeration, and now want the entire country to live according to MegaCorps' credo.

We don't feel obligated to adopt any of their values since those are based on economic concurrence, competition, singularity of their production which depend on a fluctuant market. Meaning, corporate values are based on, depend on, are contingent on an economic reality. If tomorrow a product stopped bringing in money, that company would have to fire people to survive. Consequently, the so-called corporate's values would fly away on the back of our pink slip. Will we have to adopt new ones when working for another corporation? It just doesn't make sense.

We don't want to be isolated, separated from values we share with our family, friends, common to all people from our nation. *"There is no humanist, progressivism or democratic Values crisis, there is a Neo-Liberal-Economic global absence of social values. Any ersatz of it from corporate culture won't do for the American people."* (USDF) The issue here is that MegaCorps need and want to invade and control the field of ethics which is a necessity if you want to justify an anti-democratic 'coup' to take over a society. They need to convince the citizenry that they have or can create some values which reach the finality of an ethic of transcendence. For that they need all the help the 'useful idiots' can bring by destroying our values. Naturally, here also, the control of the infosphere/media is crucial to show how great their ideas are. Without it they don't have a chance.

CEOs ARE IN THE STARTING BLOCK OF 2024 ELECTION

It is not good for the left to be caught between MegaCorps, with their obscene amounts of money and the Republican party which is draining what's left of the center left. Our party must do some serious soul searching and come up with a political program which makes sense for the citizenry. Otherwise, the door will be wide open in 2024 for Mega corps. Nobody with a sound mind would want them in charge.

We know why the info/media complex is so important

to control the citizenry, but it also helps to dominate the legislative, the executive and the judicial.

"The simplest and most efficient way to control any country is to finance the election of people who want to be elected." (USDF) You pay for their election and you own them! They will become your employees. Clearly, not all elected people are on MegaCorp's payroll. It is the ones who are benefitted by support from the media owned by corporations. Also, political NGO and lobbies, which are paid to represent their interests, are pressuring our elected officials relentlessly to advance the interests of their clients. This does not include Doctors without Borders, D.A.V. or other charitable organizations which are perfectly legitimate, and we must support them.

The old "What is good for GM is good for America" is obsolete. Now what's good for Google is good for Google only. For some SuperConglos America is a small part of their economic activity. The North American segment, including Canada, of the global market of Coca-Cola represented, in 2016, 15.4% of it 41.86 billion operating revenue business. [11] So why do we want them to give a hoot about America, since they are making their money somewhere else? *That is the key to understanding why they don't care about American people but still need to own/control our country to use it as a political weapon against other economic interests"* (USDF).

NOTES

1. mediamoussearchive.worldpress.com, Bill Clinton signed the Telecommunication Act, in 1996. It is the right place to mention that Ronald Reagan removed

the FCC "Fairness Doctrine", 1949-1987, a rule which obliged media to offer the right to answer to anybody who requested it. The polarization of our political life comprises some fallout from it.

2. Williamson, Cambridge University Press, 2015. See also, Niall Ferguson, The Ascent of Money, a Financial History of the World, Penguin Press 2008, further, Fernand Braudel, Wheels of Commerce, Civilization and Capitalism, University of California Press, 1992

3. In his dissent in Mayer's Vs. United States -272, us, 52, 293- "the doctrine of separation of powers...was adopted by the convention of 1787 but to preclude the arbitrary exercise of powers", Reinhold Niebuhr, The Irony of American History, University of Chicago, p. 23.

4. Capital in the Twenty-First Century, Will the twenty-first Century be even more inegalitarian than the nineteenth, if it is not already so? Editions du Seuil, 2013

5. Ellen Brown, seekingalpha.com, May 27, 2018.

6. We asked some English friends about the privatization of their Social Security and Railroad Co. Well, they aren't happy at all with the results and we must remember that the financial situation of 1973 England was much better than ours today

7. The front page (which since might have changed) from Le Monde newspaper, quote from Sunday NYT, January 26, 2020

8. Mr. Schultz has since officialized his candidacy for the presidency. But his SuperConglos' colleagues shunted him down. They convinced him 2020 was much too early. 2024 will offer a much better opportunity.)

9. Mr. and Mrs. Benioff just bought Time Magazine from Meredith Corp; and naturally said they will never be involved in the editorial decisions. It simply confirms that the Super-Capitalists aren't going to let ONE media be independent, also let's mention Mrs. Lauren Powell-Jobs, Steve Jobs' widow, who bought the Atlantic.

10. A company employee's salary represents an average of 70% of the expenses. So, since there are more and more trained women on the job market, companies can fire men, who end up in unemployment and they pay women 20% less. It's a very good move from a business standpoint. Still, the Badfem will see it as another proof of male sexism!

11. [Statista>topics>Coca-Cola-company]

CONCLUSION

WE ARE AWARE of some imperfections on our Essay. They reflect the extreme diversity of people involved in the writing of it. Still, hope that our book clarifies a few issues between the center left, the framework of our party and the radical fringe of the society. We don't have any issues with feminists, minorities or homosexuals. They, we, all bring something of consequence, substantial and meaningful to society. We can disagree between us on some matters, but it is part of a normal exchange of opinions. Unfortunately, we must face the tragic political consequences of Badfeminism, sexualism and radical racism of mini-minorities. Their narcissism (NPD) and political dogmatism are the base of their opinions built on manipulation and a crass ignorance of basic sociology and history. But the infosphere wants us to conform to their new reality based on those outlandish claims since it said it is! *"Well, it looks like some media people, bored with reality, work very hard at creating a fake one for us. It is not one group more than the other which is responsible; it is the systemic sum of all of them which created that social distortion where American people can't recognize their own country."* (USDF).

We are in favor of protecting the "margin" of our society from too much involvement from the government; and in exchange we expect the fringe to not interfere massively in the work of society. Somebody didn't respect that deal, and it is the fringe. The Casus Belli from the Badfem, who are a small minority of the feminist movement, the sexualists, certainly don't represent the sexuality of our society, and the radical racist minorities are all part of the social edge; nonetheless they engross the Infosphere/media with only their concerns. One of the characteristics of liberalism and democracy is that it is slow to react to abuses by virtue of tolerance for everybody. But it is a big mistake to think that it is impotent or irresolute when facing a threat to its fundamental values.

The issue here is that much of the population doesn't have to accept, and make ours, any claims from those belligerent, hostile mini minorities.

They all self-appoint themselves as the bearers of some new moral standard we must consent to. But whatever they write, say etc. won't resolve any societal issues by reason of the absence of a common structural core of values which can emerge only when you combine the need of the full society. They don't have any ideological coherence. Their only point in common is distaste, hostility, malevolence toward the society in which they live. It creates dissension and divisiveness for all of us. There is nothing about the common good in their proposal. Their narcissist pitiful little tap dance around their Me-Me-Me claims for special treatment won't do.

All human beings are responsible to rescue, assist, support, comfort any other human being regardless of their gender, sexuality, skin color, religion etc. Our open society must remain so and reject any system of beliefs organized around a core of dogmatic assumptions which are absolute only for the RRM. We didn't accept it from different religions, different schools of thought, political parties. Our society, due to its size and diversity of people, is built upon a set of 'Values set at a Minima' which is agreeable to all. Democracy can work its wonders thanks to it. Why do the Badfem, the sexualists or the RRM, the infosphere and SuperConglos think we should comply?

The mini-minorities' world is socially very small. An individual is a scared person who sees threats to integrity from everywhere, from everybody, etc. Therefore, their reflex is to pile up even more dogmatism, racism, parochialism, etc. We saw that *"they go as far as recasting what they consider their "ideology" into their identity"* (USDF). The trick is for them to look bigger than they are by flapping their little wings very hard trying to occupy more social space. This is where the media echo chamber is so useful to them.

Do we have to vote for someone because she is a 'woman' and of 'color', (in her case it's a double whammy), or because a white man's credential is being homosexual, married to another man, or a candidate heterosexual white woman who underlines in her program that the highest level of her administration will be 'open', 'reserved' to, not homosexual, but 'LGBTQ+++'. Well, the color of your skin, your gender, or your sexuality isn't for us a proof of competence and intelligence. The leadership's game plan of those RRM/lobbies is to collect as many votes as they can under gender, sexual or racial identity and use it as a bargaining chip to advance their specific programs. The cherry on top, of course, would be playing the king makers. This is a wrong evolution of our democracy. It's lobbyism going berserk in the democratic electoral process.

All the people from the RRM crowd completely lost the sense of measure, of critical thinking, of analytical capacity, and worst of all, rationality and that is catastrophic for everybody, them included. They just don't know it yet.

Us from the good left, we won't stay stuck with them in that kind of rhetoric--full of resentment against everybody who doesn't share their view. We say to them, you are free to think; be whatever you want, but stay away from our values of humanism, progressive-liberalism and democracy, since they are the bedrock of our society.

Not all claims for the status of 'social value' are legitimate. To have it, it must pass a series of litmus tests, the most important one being: Is that new Value beneficial to our society? We can say that consumerism, gender racism, sexualism, greed, misandrist, racism, misogyny etc. aren't passing that test. So, if people in favor of it insist on shoving it down our throats, we should push them, gently first, toward the 'garbage of history'. Why?

Because people like us want to live in an environment where fairness, loyalty, spirituality, respect, discipline, achievement, love, etc. are recognized for what they are: necessities that we always must keep our focus on to upgrade our inadequate, deficient human condition. All those good values must be part of 'an ethic of convictions' which imply 'an ethic of responsibility' in each of us. All of us, of any color, religion, etc. are all in the same boat. The Covid-19 pandemic remind us of that basic fact of life on this planet. We welcome any good debates, heated discussions, objective criticisms, virulent controversies which are part of any social life in a free society; but at the end we must make some agreement, to make our society a better place to live for all of us.

Our country has just a few tools such as taxes, education, social solidarity to keep our society together. Let's rehabilitate completely our public educational system and use it as the melting pot it used to be; and not forget public health, our infrastructure, etc. Let's educate all young people and give them a chance to be the best they can be, to share true and moral values. But can we, when our social lives are based on falsity, distortion, and deception by people whose only goals are the 2020 or 2024 elections? But to try to make Latino, white or Asian people feel guilty about 1619 is a really poor strategy based on a total disregard of what Americans, who grew up watching Roots and Prince of Bel Air, are. They aren't buying that story that they all are racist pigs, who need to be reminded that they are the descendants of plantation owners! To cover up our problems with a racist thematic drastically limits our message, but do we have one besides the made up one from RRM?

Now let's recapitulate what the 800-pound gorilla is up to. Regarding the infosphere/medias/complex, we understand now why SuperConglos need and support all those radical minorities, and how useful they are to divert people from real and urgent problems. The 'useful idiots' are around to hide the SuperCapital nihility of values and to pit women against men, black against white, homosexual against heterosexual, poor against poor, believers against non-believers, poor against rich, majority against minority, etc.

Nothing new, it's just the old 'divide and conquer' stratagem. They always think they are so intelligent, so strong, so rich they can keep 'people' under control. But history shows us, to play the divisiveness card, is a very dangerous political game. They can lose control of those groups very quickly; since they are irrational and unpredictable, due to the volatility of their ideas which already opened the door to several strains of social react-evolution, populism, racism, ghettoization etc. All of those are building an unstable underground for our society.

The super-brains of Silicon Valley are naked now. Everything we knew was coming is here. Millions and millions of American citizens are facing identity theft, have their information used mercilessly, their private life exposed and exploited by, not the government, the police, or a dictator etc. but by private corporations. What we were so afraid of from communism, from big government is now right here in our society and it is the result of work done by some dangerously irresponsible American economic social forces which refuse adamantly any regulations, when they are responsible for creating that mess in the first place. And now those people want to govern us? But why? So far, we see them accumulating an insane amount of power and money. For what purpose? It's certainly not to improve the welfare of the people.

How valid is their commitment to Democracy? We

are very suspicious about the intentions of that small, elitist ruling class, who intend to govern without the "check and balance" of equality, freedom and justice. We have a first-class country. We elected Republicans and Democrats and they have the obligation to keep freedom and all our democratic institutions alive; whatever their political differences are. They must work together because what WE are facing is the greatest threat to our freedom, since it's coming from a very powerful group of interests inside our society.

The E.U., Chinese, Russians etc. aren't the cause of our extreme political polarization, neither are they responsible for the fact that we have lurking in ambush, in our financial arcane, trillions and trillions in deficits

The reality is we live in a multi-polar world, with an insane arsenal, and we can predict that every country, will rush back behind their borders trying to save furniture, in case of major crisis. Globalization or not, nobody will have a choice. Therefore, we must pay attention to the latent underlying conflicts, from Erdogan in the Mediterranean/Middle East area, to Pakistan/India/China in Kashmir etc. which could evolve into large arm conflict because some countries won't be able to survive behind their borders and war is always a good opportunity to find a solution to internal problems. What will be SuperConglos course of action since they have economic interests in every country? Which side will they choose? We must, we have the obligation to keep an eye on those people.

How do we dare! Well, because it will be our democratic state which will save the day again and it is doing it right now. Let's look at our financial 'elite' rushing to

Uncle Sam to save their ass-ets. We are smart enough not to kill the 'Golden Goose's MegaCorps, which brings progress, but instead a *few* giant ones which control everything, including us. We want a multitude of them, smaller but much more dynamic, focusing on their goals which are economic development. We need to reintroduce the market dynamism at the highest level of our economy. *"The fights, with billion upon billion, between economic titans aren't an expression of a healthy market economy. It is in fact exactly the opposite; it is a fight between them for political power"* (USDF).

And if globalization requires the existence of Super-Corporations to compete at the global level, we should help them with our strong institutions elected by the people who will make sure that the common good is respected. We want the polity, the sovereignty, of the republic back in the saddle making sure that no CEO, board of directors, lobbies, etc. can overwrite any of our values, any of our laws. Businesspeople should be busy with their businesses and working with us, not against us, to make the changes necessary to have an efficient political apparatus. We don't want to go back to the past. We need to rebuild our democracy on a much better framework of responsibility, power and democratic control of all our political institutions; and go all together toward a 'glorious future'.

Democracy: a system of government in which power is vested in the people, who rule either directly or through freely elected representatives, and the content of democracy is composed of values agreed upon by the people.

"Democracy is like a coin with two sides, one side is Democrat and the other is Republican, and both are equally responsible for its value." (USDF).

We were able to live under that umbrella for a few centuries, weren't we? It is urgent to reintroduce the ballots. When advancing new laws, we must ask people their preference. We may be surprised how smart people are when you inform them properly, when you explain honestly the ins and outs of an issue. Nobody should disparage the citizenry. It is them, we, who are living with, or under those laws and we have the fundamental right to choose the way we want to live. We won't let anybody take that right from us.

We aren't saying every decision must go through referendum or ballot, but when you change some fundamental values you must go through the process of popular vote.

We need to elect people of character, intelligence and competence because the situation is dire and unstable. It will be difficult since we will have a plethora of fabricated, mock candidacies propped up by the media to keep us in an illusion of a democratic debate! Unfortunately, we don't have many interesting candidates to offer. A complete generation of leaders is missing. They were snuffed by the Clintons' political machine.

Some of us think that our party is in very bad shape. Can it salvage itself with the same team that led to 2016? We must offer an alternative to the American people. If one party is missing the internal political balance, the dialectic between a Democrat and Republican dynamic ceases to exist. In the actual situation, our party is unable to defend Democracy from those negative social forces we expose in our book.

Americans are tired of seeing and hearing pharisaic impostors of all creeds claiming they are in favor of democracy and at the same time trying to remove "due process" from our judicial system. It probably explain why 41% of voters are registered as independent, why we had exceptional voters participation and Donald Trump able to amass 10 more millions votes when losing the election... all that in 2020! It could be an opportunity to create something new. Let's think and talk, American people from both sides are resourceful, don't underestimate them!

We, us, the group, think that Walt Whitman got it right when he wrote "the purpose of democracy, isn't wealth, or even equality, it is the full flowering of individuals," because that individual, thanks to equality, will get an education, become more open and intelligent, more creative, productive and our society will get fairer, richer because it's full of talents, which are the base of the exceptional development of modern societies. We say to people busy piling up billion over billion, trying to rebuild a feudal society, don't touch democracy, don't try to raze it to the ground. Your power comes from the incredible capacity of the human being to think and create and that, thanks to the Freedom that only democracy--its values and norms protect and guarantee! Somehow, there is a little voice in our heads which says that America, despite all its shortcomings, is a great nation and that, overall, the Western Civilization is first rate. We are in favor of improving it, making it progress, making it better for all of us.

From the Nothingness of our birth to the Nothingness of our death we have the Cartesian Cogito, "I think therefore I am," and all of us are floating, more or less, in a space where our rationality, religious beliefs, humanist convictions are like life saver rings which structure our identity. We have Freedom, call it free will if you want, which allows us to choose to belong to a country, a church, a political party, to act decently, even heroically, or, since we are human, stupidly. Humanism is fundamental to progressive-liberalism and democracy by giving all of us the opportunity to make our own decisions, where ALL human beings are in solidarity to build a future. It is an incredible story. And all that because we must remember that millions and millions of people died for us, to make sure we live in a free country. We would like to give the same courtesy to our children and let all future generations live peacefully in a Democratic society. It's the least we can do.

Our last words on the subject? *"The liberty of a democracy is not safe if the people tolerated the growth of private power to a point where it becomes stronger than the Democratic State itself. That in its essence is fascism."* Franklin D. Roosevelt.

The end, that's all folks

ADDENDUMS FEMINISM

About Stormy Daniels

We are using the following case only because the woman was very explicit about it. Stormy Daniels, during an interview with Anderson Cooper said she wasn't at all attracted by Donald Trump but had sex with him anyway (without condom – she is allergic to latex). So, she doesn't use condoms and had sex willingly with that very powerful man that she isn't attracted to. She was never under any obligation to have sex with him, NEVER. *"Where are the books from the Badfem, explaining women's inconsistency, the discrepancy between their fancy and the meaning of their choice at the sexual level, about their fascination with power, sex, fame and money, because it does exist in the real world. Women have sex with men for very different reasons and certainly not always because of love, basically like men!"* (USDF)

About Patriarchy

The traditional family structure and its corollary, Patriarchy, was smashed by industrialization in the mid-19th Century. Among the consequences of that destruction we saw a vast increase of prostitution, alcoholism, etc. So, far from us the idea to criticize women and men who fought hard to reestablish some sense of decency in city life, since the traditional family structure centered around the small farm, shop, wasn't able anymore to support a complete family. First the father left, followed soon by sons and daughters to join the army of workers necessary for the Industrial Revolution. So, the patriarch jumped from his glorious perch to another perch supposedly as glorious, by becoming an hourly paid worker.

About share custody

The NOW movement could have fostered, encouraged shared custody in case of divorce. It was so important to help women by shoring up men to their children, to make them responsible for them. It was possible, if you had educated men and women in a new way of living, of sharing responsibility. But we repeat, education is a detestation, an anathema for Badfem. Now, we have an insane number of women raising children alone, victim of Bad-fems first-class incompetence.

A FEW BOOKS THAT WE RECOMMAND

We consulted a few books: Ellen Messer-Davidow, *From Social Activism to Academic Discourse: The New Feminist Agenda,* Duke University Press, 2002; Madeline Kunin, *The New Feminist Agenda: Defining the Next Revolution for women, Work Family,* Chelsea Green Publishing, 2012; Laura Kipnis, *Men: Notes from an Ongoing Investigation,* Picador Print, 2015; Jessa Crispin, *Why I am not a Feminist: Feminist Manifesto,* Melville House, 2017.

About human shortcomings

We must accept the idea that both men and women are human beings and that their shortcomings aren't due to their sex but to their humanity. The magic words in a relationship between them are partnership, synergy, respect, compromise, give and take, love, etc. If the number of women raising children on their own is absurd, we must notice that the number of households headed by men jumped from 1% in the 1960s to 10% in 2013. (source: Gretchen Livingston, *The Rise of Single Fathers*, July 2, 2013.) In both cases, we don't see any improvement. If you have children, it is not the responsibility of the State or the government but of people who created them. The rights and responsibility must be shared equally between the creators of a new life. Regarding children, the government must be involved only in helping educationally and in public health, because it is in its interest to have a well-educated, productive citizenry in good health. It has nothing to do with welfare or charity. Everybody, in any society, can take advantage of it--especially the capital which benefits greatly to have a well-educated work force. Needless to say, SuperConglos will prefer to take care of it. They will educate people only for their economic needs. The rest will be a mass of half-instructed people laboring in the lower strata of the society.

The reality of women being equal to men implies that they are as great, and able as men. Right? Some_women should stop being delusional about the reality of their own sex. A woman prime minister said, "Whether women are better than men I cannot say - but they are certainly no worse" (Golda Meir). It is our final word on the matter. (source: Marty Klein, book, *America's information about war on sex, The Continuing Attack on Lust, Law, and Liberty*, Second Edition, Praeger, 2012, gave us a lot of information.)

About Simone De Beauvoir and Shulamith Firestone

It is time for us to give Badfem a taste of their own medicine. About invading the privacy of all our self-appointed vigilant guardian of our personal lives. But we don't look through peepholes, making judgments on other humans when in fact we don't know anything about them. So, let's give Taliban-rat-Badfem two examples of what we can write about any of them if we decide to. Naturally, we can do the same to all creepy journalists from the 'creepy press'!

Let's talk about one of their goddesses: Simone de Beauvoir, who was bi-sexual and a teacher, expelled from the French School system, for "sexually abusing" one of her underage female students. She was a writer, existentialist but never considered herself as a serious philosopher like Jean Paul Sartre, but a writer and political activist. Now, we call people like that lesbian/bi, with a very strong emphasis on lesbianism. She was into young women, and not always in a nice way. Living in a beautiful neighborhood in Paris, she never had any children, though married to Jean Paul Sartre on a 'Let's sign a two-year lease to get rid of our parents' and practicing open marriage! Well, according to our Badfem, Simone was an expert on women's issues. We must let them know that a large majority of American women are scratching their heads, trying to figure out where Simone got her understanding and knowledge of what being a woman and mother in the real world is.

It also appears to us that another Badfem intellectual beacon was suffering from serious mental illness. Shulamith Firestone, author of *The Dialectic of Sex* was much closer to Asimov than to Betty Friedan. Why didn't Badfem ask the editor of her books to let the readers know that she spent quite a lot of time in mental institutions? For us, human life is messy and hard to handle; and certainly, doesn't deserve that all-out war on people's private lives. The war against sexual abuses by SOME men and women? We are part of it, since our boys, girls, wives, husbands, friends can be victims of it! But nothing, absolutely nothing, justifies the Badfem's creation of hysteria by making EVERY man a sexual predator, wife abuser, incestuous father, misogynist, sexist pig, etc. and that for more than half a century.

We chose De Beauvoir and Firestone on purpose because their privacy won't be affected by what we wrote since both are deceased.

About Intersectionality, another wooden theory of bad feminism

Were we really surprised to see Senator Kristen Gillibrand using it in her campaign? Not really, because she used to belong to Hilary's Badfem's posse and those people were very, very strong on deconstructivism which opened the door to all sorts of theories. Intersectionality is just one of them.

To simplify, it is an idea that gender, race, sexuality, age, religion, classism, skin color, etc. (put in it anything you want) are hinged together through different social layers. It's a tentative idea designed to create a reticulation between political claims, mostly issuing from mini minorities who try to give to themselves some political weight and volume they don't have on their own.

But, piling up assertions and demands doesn't create a coherent political program with which to work. You just create a huge, in that case media, blob of contradictions that nobody can use. It is a really poor version of the 'Inter Culture" theory in German philosophy (see, as an introduction to it, Bernhard Siegert, *Cultural Techniques: Or the End of the Intellectual Postwar Era in German Media Theory*, tcs.sagepub.com) To regroup all unhappy RRMs under intersectionality won't resolve any problems since there is some fundamental political contradictions between them, their claims and interests. It is at best an open-shut of medley of beliefs trying to make the LHBTQ+++, which has for goal to change our definition of human sexual life, to be a bedfellow with, with BLM Michael Dyson which want trillion and trillion of $ for some RRM. Both claims are too divergent to make sense.

So, Mrs. Gillibrand, an able Senator, chose as a political motto: our future is: female intersectionality powered by belief in one another. And she wants to create a movement call Moral Restoration in America because "... that's the biggest impediment we have in Washington are these circles and the system of power that have been in place for a very long time that will not loosen their grip, and that power is based on corruption and greed." We must face those issues, but to bring back an updated version, from the 1920s, of the most spectacular political failures of feminism as a solution to our actual problem is baffling to us. Any political solution based on a rehash of the good old-time moral restoration based on RRM' claims is a non-starter. Too bad, Mrs. Gillibrand could have been a good presidential candidate. (see Benjamin Wallace-Wells, Kristen Gillibrand and the new face of moral reform, March 8, 2019.)

About toxic male privileges

We have another example to give about misguided politic by some woman. A famous singer thinks that a business contract is just a worthless piece of paper since she is victim of "toxic male privilege" by those who own the contracts. We expected better from Taylor Swift, a talented, savvy, qualified and very rich businesswoman. It is her choice to jump on the bandwagon of Badfem's victimhood. She can stay in it as far as we are concerned. Her 'toxic male privilege' is badly outworn. She shouldn't be a wuss, and actually call it what it is: a ferocious fight between her (corporation) and some other corporations, over the control of hundreds of millions of $! It happens every day in our country and nobody is whining about it and calling for the sympathy of their fans! Can we lend a helping hand and refer her to 'A Brief History of the Ownership of the Beatles Catalog', (Dan Rys, billboard.com, 1-20-2017) She must know that Michael Jackson, at one point, had a controlling interest in the Beatles catalogue, always refused to sell it back to Paul McCartney, who just started a lawsuit against Sony which now controls it. So, Ms. Swift's use of the 'toxic male privilege' is pure sophistry and deception.

About unequal pay claims

Badfem's statistics and data regarding equal pay are regularly contradicted by studies not motivated by any political agenda. We saw previously how crafty at using deceit and lies they are to manipulate the public with that most ludicrous disinformation that women make 30% less than men. When we look at Wikipedia's numbers, it arrives at around 6% of salary discrepancy. Some other studies bring the number to 3%. The statistician's tools can't explain why a difference of 3% persists. But why such a difference of 30% between the Badfem's numbers and other significant research? And why, when you compare oranges to oranges, men and women doing the same job, same number of hours, same number of years, for the same company are they paid the same? Our question is why the infosphere/media keeps hammering Badfem's agitprop-(aganda). Well, because politically that bamboozle is very useful for both sides. The media buy for cheap some fake progressivism, 'we defend the victims' and the Badfem protect their 'victimhood' brainwashing in the social discourse. They are scratching each other's back. (source: Rosin, *The End of Men and the Rise of Women,* Riverhead Books, 2012. Karin Agness Lips, don't buy into the gender gap myth, forbes.com, April 12,2016. Ashe Schow, *Harvard Professor Takes Down Gender Gap Myth,* Washington Examiner, January 13, 2016.)

About Slavery, reminder of a few basic facts.

* The Census of 1860 registered 32% of white family-owned black slaves in the South, if we

include the total population living in America, the percentage goes down to 1.4% of people who owned slaves. Everybody in our group think that slavery was ghastly, horrendous and you can't justify it. But where does the "collective guilt of white people" come from?

* 245 years of selling humans is atrocious according to our modern standard of living. Well, it is very brief in comparison to the millenniums of such practice by all societies from Africa, the Middle East, Asia, Europe. Our country certainly didn't invent slavery!

* In 'the good old days' human life didn't have any value. You could kill as many men as you wanted, always keeping women alive for their reproductive capacity!

* Only 6% of the twelve to fifteen Million of transplanted Africans went to the United States.

* Free black, Indians, Latino and other minorities owned black slaves.

* Some white people exploited slavery.

* Some white people dismantled slavery.

* White people killed each other, making a moral principle triumph over ignorance and social injustice.

About violence in our Society

Violence is swelling all over our society and the response has been increased militarization of the police, wearing reinforced, bullet proof vests to arrest two low-level young drug dealers, equipped with AK47s, which are real war weapons. If we are looking for an explanation for why cops have their fingers on the trigger, look no further than this. The New Yorker published a 12-page article describing the consequences of drugs, racism, and incompetence for breeding violence. (source: Ben Taub, The Spy who Came Home, why an expert in counterterrorism became a beat cop, The New Yorker, May 7, 2018) The interview with Patrick Skinner is explicitly about the police officers who are picking up the pieces of "... something that has broken in every possible way" and trying to fix it "... usually without adequate training and, often without the skills they need, and overwhelmingly without the resources and institutional connections that it would take to do those things well." That might mean putting an unstable person into a public mental health facility, instead of a cell. Cops aren't nurses, or social workers, or psychologists. We call them in case of crimes like robbery, domestic violence, or murder. Guns are one of their tools; they have no obligation to give CPR to somebody who overdoses in the middle of a public park. That is the responsibility of paramedics and social workers. However, those departments are badly understaffed, because most of our cities can't afford to adequately support them. Facilities that care for social problems are mostly in such bad shape, they're closed or virtually useless.

In Baltimore, after the riots, criminality increased because arrests went down 20%. Cops, all colors included, refused to patrol the most lawless, toughest areas, leaving the poor neighborhoods even more exposed to all forms of violence. People from 'Cure violence' or 'Interceptor violence' make desperate efforts in those neighborhoods to limit the social impact of violence on the population. It is those people who need our help.

About respecting the laws

When people crash a private pool party to get free drinks, harass women, bully men, etc. we call the police, but cops show up in a situation where violence is already well established. Before blaming the cops let's take a good look at ourselves!

If Eric Garner, that poor fellow, had followed the instruction of moving out of the spots where he was standing, he would be alive today. A merchant started things by issuing a complaint that Garner must be removed from the area. It was the confrontation with the cops which ended with a choke hold (illegal practice in the NYPD) for around 15 to 19 seconds. He didn't die from it. But the piling up of six cops on him certainly affected his capacity to breathe especially since he was asthmatic, overweight, had cardio-vascular diseases and was 6.3 feet tall. More than eleven times we can hear him saying "I can't breathe." What a heartbreaking story about somebody who had just minor brushes with the law before for selling "loosies," cigarettes by the unit, on the street. Please don't die for something like that! Follow the police instructions and leave the scene. But why did he look for a confrontation with the cops?

Now, some are equipped with bodycams and were able to prove that a woman from a minority, complaining that she had been anal and vaginally penetrated by officers, was just a liar from A to Z. The advantage of filming an incident from the beginning has a great advantage over those phone videos which are activated after an incident started.

Violence is increasing all over our society and it is not the right time to ask America to abandon self-defense, in view of the fact, that, and we insist, it is going to get much worse before getting better. The latest claim from incompetent radicals to defund the police is a good reminder of how our situation has become fraught with incertitude. We must now put security guards with guns in temples and churches to protect people worshiping God, in schools, at social events etc. TV shows like "Cops" give us plenty of examples of brutality, roughness of people when dealing with police. Do we think that a drunk, a druggy on meth, an armed criminal is interested in a peaceful solution? They will choose to put a bullet in the head of a police officer, married with five children (Jersey City shootout, New Jersey, 12-10-19) instead of having a peaceable conversation with him.

Democrat or Republican agree, 86 to 84%, to have regulations regarding access to guns. Why can't we make an agreement between both sides?

Probably because of the unresolved central question which is, who is going to control the registration of guns? The government, the police are claiming the Democrats. It isn't tolerable say the Republicans because any government from the right or the left can disarm the citizenry and install a dictature in the blink of an eye. It is a threat that, from the Founding Fathers to now, we must face. Not one of the three branches of or government should be fully trusted to have access to the information of all citizens who own guns. Can we suggest the creation of a neutral structure, independent of any political interferences, a structure, an organization in charge of keeping track of registration that, only after an injunction from a judge, can the police consult to track down murderers, gun running etc.? Positive and sensible suggestions are welcome. If we resolve the issue of gun registration, a dialogue will be possible between the two sides which agree on the need of legislation.

About affirmative action and racism.

A discriminatory and racist system of selection, and to call it "adversity score" won't change anything in that reality.

To justify the concept of whiteness they have a claim based on 'knapsack of privileges' that only Whites have. A person of color, accepted to an Ivy League school, with 1,060 SATs, when at the same time a student, with a 1,600, from a modest social background, is turned down, because he is white and a male, isn't, according to RRM, a big privilege. Well, it is. That quota system, by its structural definition, limiting access to higher education to Asians and Whites, is racist. It is a similar story as the quota imposed on Jews before the sixties, because there were too many of them in higher education. Now some Asians, who are following the path of education, are suing Harvard because they are victims of discrimination. (see Hua Hsu, Schools Colors, Will an alliance between Asian-American activists and white conservatives end affirmative Action? The New Yorker. October 15, 2018.)

We try desperately to squeeze minorities into higher education. It is the wrong politic; it won't reduce social disparity in meritocracy. We must reverse that dynamic and enlarge drastically higher education and create new establishments as elitist as the one already existing, with a selection based on academic results. We mean more Brown, U of C, Princeton, Stanford, MIT, Harvard, etc. We need to increase the magnitude of our elite! We must start from the base, the ground floor of our educational system. We must give equal access to education for everybody according to their aptitude, from apprentice to doctorate. It's critical because the general level of education for American people went down for the last thirty years. It is the first time in our history. We need a huge mass of educated people. It is the bottom line for the survival of our country. The place to start is with that nationwide day care system we mention in the introduction. It will be the foundation of an infrastructure totally dedicated to permanent education, owing to the fact that we will likely change occupations, jobs during our lifetime and we must get ready.

All children, youngsters, teenagers, students must have access to it. A lot of that infrastructure already exists. To reach that goal we must give our teachers the support they need, train them the right way, pay them a decent salary and invest in facilities. No private charity can assume such an enormous task. Our goal isn't to create a monstrous department of education but to create a 'strategic master plan' that both parties must support, independently of which one is in power. All private institutions, charter schools, etc. will be more than welcome to bring their competence. The system we think of is flexible, adaptable and able to identify, recognize, all along the schooling period, children with capacity. The scholastic standard will be the one opening the door to higher education, not the color of your skin, your family background, or the prejudice of any member on a selection board. Our proposal will work only if education becomes a primary concern in our culture. We must stop losing million and millions of "good brains" from minorities and majorities.

About what civilization means

Race-based theories have been abandoned by nearly everybody. But not by the RRM, who insists that there is a White race and if you are white you are a racist; meaning that you are racist because you are white; and since Whites are the majority, America is racist, right?

Meaning if the first-class Chinese and Muslim civilizations were dominant it would be because they were racist?

We disagree. Chinese and Muslim civilizations were first class, at their time, because of the superiority of their culture, social organization, scientific discoveries. The RRM must know that Judeo-Christianity, Greek philosophy, Enlightenment philosophy, scientific discoveries, are the foundation of Western Civilization and we don't intend to apologize for the greatness of it! All the focusing on its shortcomings by the RRM won't change anything to that reality. Badfeminism, RRM, sexualists think that snarling at who they perceive as enemies will give them the philosophical stone necessary to resolve their troubles. They want to ignore 1775 (American Revolution), 1789 (French Revolution), 1917 (Russian Revolution) which affected the evolution of the planet.

ADDENDUMS INFOSPHERE/MEDIA

About mass shooting

Are the ultimate residual of a social culture in decay! When we look around us, we see an increase of social violence, murders, suicides, rapes, drugs, abuses and aggressiveness everywhere. It is the background from which mass murderers arise. There is nothing in their life which gives them justification to keep living. A human being isn't just an animal looking for its next meal. It is a highly sociable creature, but the last thirty years our society is evolving more and more toward individualism, competition, rivalry, etc. which have resulted in increased isolation and loneliness. For some people it creates so much anxiety that it splinters their identity, which brings catastrophic psychological consequences. From there they can commit suicide, mass murders, etc. They will turn out to be the animal engendered by a society which sacrificed human solidarity, basic values, and public mental health.

Let's look at a few cases.

A young married man with some mental problems, and an addiction to steroids killed over 50 people in a homosexual bar.

In Santa Barbara, another young man, who also had serious mental problems toward the female gender killed six people. The journalists saw here an exemplary cause of misogynism without noticing he killed more men than women! Well, we have to suppose he was an incompetent misogynist!

In Dayton, Ohio, a man killed nine people, including his own sister.

Another, who was sleeping in his car, unemployed, on food stamps, went to a super store to have lunch, changed his mind, got a weapon from his car and killed 20 people at random in the store--most of them Latinos. It happened in south Texas.

In Gilroy, they found the 19-year-old killer's targets list: religious institutions, federal buildings, courthouse and the garlic festival. Yes, the garlic festival! "Why are you doing this?" asked a witness. "Because I am angry," was his response! There is no logic, no meaningful ideology in that answer. A 16-year-old teenager killed people and shot himself in the head on his birthday! (Happy birthday, kiddo!) All those people just try, in a last desperate act, to give meaning to what they perceive as their meaningless lives. It can go as far as someone seemingly ordinary in Las Vegas, a well-off middle-aged white man with a nice girlfriend. The man didn't even bother to justify killing over 57 people! Not a word, not a note to explain why. It was probably not worth it for him.

Anyone getting a call stating that your child, your mate, your friend has been killed is for all of us the ultimate horror. We want to make sense of those tragedies. We are desperate to find an explanation. What is the motivation behind those shootings? Misogyny?

About Infosphere/media

- Google represents 90% of search traffic.
- IHeartCommunications.inc., formerly Clear Channel Communications, owns over 1,207 stations Radio, average of 25 Radio Stations per State, 1,400. Worldwide, 39 TV Stations

- Facebook represents 85% of social traffic.
- Amazon has 75% of all e-book sales.

If some people think that nobody, especially the people who control it, won't use such an awesome power however they wish, they are mistaken. [5]

About information and education

One of the characteristics of authoritarianism is that nobody is ever responsible - Adolf Eichmann, since he was in the system, never considered himself responsible for anything. It was based on the constant credo of any ruling interests which is 'let us be in charge, since everything is well beyond your comprehension'. They think we will buy that kind of self-serving nonsense. What should we do? They expect us to take a stick and go beat an algorithm silly.

Let's start by making the authors and manufacturers of those identify their creative designs. It should be public knowledge if we want to pinpoint who is responsible for some really bad consequences of their products, like we have a Vin number for our cars.

The Millennials already grow up in that world and think, since they have an unlimited access to information, that they know what's going on everywhere. There is no reason to blame them; they have no training in handling that tremendous amount of information thrown at them. *"This is why we insist on the school system to start educating young people on how to use the infosphere with a 'cultural strainer'; to get rid of the meaningless, select the significant, and connect the dots between the worthwhile, the substantial and eliminate the worthless"* (USDF). If we don't, it will be the triumph of alt-facts which can create a virtual reality for millions and millions of people. They will vote according to their perception of what they think is reality when in fact it is not! They will be under the control of the media and its masters, think, the Wizard of OZ!

(See WSJ.com, Kristen Grind, Sam Schechner, Robert McMillan and John West, How Google interferes with its search algorithms and changes your results, the Internet giant uses blacklists, algorithm tweaks and an army of contractors to shape what you see, Nov. 15, 2019)

Infosphere/media plow directly into the population's brain. So, to snatch our attention is politically crucial, since "Attention is a data handling method." and, as it happens, affects our perception of information. "Attention actually is an emergent property; it emerges from the competition among signals in the brain. Attention is a state into which information can enter our brains and we can select information and grasp the focus of our attention. Attention is not itself information. It is something that happens to information." To simplify, being aware of something isn't information. Being aware of violence doesn't include the information about why? Therefore, it is all-important for the ruling interests to grab our attention at any cost and keep it for as long as possible. Information will operate with what has grabbed our attention, where we will find very few facts about what's going on in America, but plenty of trash. (Michael S. Graziano, Consciousness and the Social Brain, Oxford University Press, 2013, p. 131.)

ADDENDUMS SUPERCONGLOS

About a little break?

In 2007, before 2008's crash, banks were offering insane house loans. One person from our group, living in Los Angeles, had excellent credit and a good positive cash account balance. He was contacted by his bank, Washington Mutual, to buy a $3,500,000 house with 1% down payment ($35,000). Happily, he passed on such a loan with a variable interest rate! The realtor, of course, thought he was a total idiot to disregard such a bargain! Over 10 million American citizens lost their homes; most of them haven't recovered from it.

About the importance of finance

We have, as citizens, the responsibility to make sure our society doesn't fly out of control. We used to have roughly a ruling class who owned stuff and a power elite which was composed of professional managers, politicians, military leaders, people of exceptional character, etc. That set up change progressively from the early '70s. Globalization of big American corporations necessitated a huge amount of money to finance all merger & acquisition required by globalization. They had to move factories and implement the new industrial/high-tech complex which goes with it, etc. As a result, the finance people received more and more power in the decision-making of our economy. Nothing wrong with it since the banks always play an important role in economy. But now the elite of that business act like they already own our country. We are nicely asking them to back off.

The opacity of the financial world is such that most of

us have no idea of who is doing what. They use a highly specialized language, techy mumbo jumbo that keeps opaque any decision taken. That way they justify their arguments that the society is far too sophisticated for us to understand. It's not prevarication, they really believe in their own falsehood. They think we should let them be in charge. That kind of fallacy works only if the public is deceived on a massive scale; but by what and whom? Well, the infosphere/media that they own. Unfortunately for them, most people still have the capacity to understand the staggering transfer of state competence and responsibility to SuperCorps, and how much it affects their lives. They deal every day with the liquidation of the concept of public service like public health. (We recommend here an essay by Nicholas Lehman, When Corporations Changed their social role – and Upended our Politics, WSJ, Sept 6, 2019. That book, *Transaction Man: The Rise of the Deal and the Decline of the American Dream*, published by Farrar, Strauss and Giroux. It explains clearly the transformation of the "concept of corporation" (Peter Drucker) from the early 20th century to the present.)

About two neo-Liberalism theories

We can apprehend neo-liberalism from the two interrelated sides of the same thesis characterized by theorists like Carl Schmidt and Friedrich Hayek. Both had a foundational impact on neo-liberal economy. They have in common an opposition to the democratic process. (we need to simplify a lot and limit our discussion to principal constituents of that theory of economics.)

Certainly rationality, science, and logic brought spectacular progress and there is nothing wrong with that. However, thinkers found that progress had, inherently, a form of determinism advance from its logic. If you take a stone and throw it at a window you will break the glass. If you do it one thousand times you will always get the same result; you can't escape it, meaning the fact of throwing a stone already carries the result of a broken window. So, this is where "Decisionism" of Carl Schmidt, (Political Theology, 1922) was derived. *"But now it is buried in the decision process of modern technology. We can witness a systematic camouflage of human responsibility under anonymous algorithms. The latest are a dream come true for management but results in cancelling any form of debate, dialogue, or scrutiny of the "decision"* (USDF).

We never see or hear of any human involved in the writing of such a tool who decides that you won't get reimbursed for a medication that keeps you alive. Anyway, why do you want to linger around when the economic logic of you being alive doesn't make sense? You are too costly! You are an anachronism in and for the economic order carried by the algorithms. You should have died a few weeks before you became a burden to the system.

So, the logic of Carl Schmidt, a German philosopher, in cahoots with the Nazis, lies in wait in the neo-liberal economic theory. It is worrisome. If you don't think so, you are on a greasy, slippery slope called fascism which has a very bad habit of being typically efficient.

Friedrich Hayek (*The Road to Serfdom*, 1944) saw firsthand the consequences of the catastrophic WWII. He was on the theoretical opposite side of the same neo-liberal economy theory as Carl Schmidt. He was among one of the most influential intellectuals of that theory. He insisted on the equality brought to all nations by the market economy's laws. Complications start when those laws enter into conflict with the one inherent to democracy and its values. However, not one economic system, traditional, market, mixed, command socialist, capitalist, archaic, etc.) can carry anything remotely concerned with societal values. As we wrote above, capitalism has its own qualities, but MegaCorps play havoc with capitalism by gaming the rules of information, market competitions, etc.

Economic laws are a product of economic activities and they coexist with any form of political government. But neo-liberals' SuperConglos understand well that democracy's laws are antagonistic to their freedom to do business the way they wish, which can be very expensive. The 2020 "neo-liberalism" responsible for the financial crack of 2008, dropped all pretense and wants now to apply their economic rules to all layers of our society. They don't need or care anymore for any fancy theories from Chicago or the London School of Economics.

Things being what they are in our country, we must focus on all the causes which bring the dreadful consequences we see all over us. We must stop putting Band-Aid on wooden legs and build a block of organizations having for goal to safeguard Democracy that all citizen Democrats, Republican of any sex, creed or color cherish dearly. We must establish a Master Plan for a multipronged defense of our Values. It will be a socio-political fight of some breadth.

In our next five books we will have proposal, suggestions open to any improvement from people concerned by the future of our country. We have a plethora of intellectually honest, intelligent people, from every side of our social life, able to create a wide platform which can bring soundness, consistency, clarity in our politic. America is a great, extremely resilient country.

www.ingramcontent.com/pod-product-compliance
Lightning Source LLC
Chambersburg PA
CBHW071349280326
41927CB00040B/2464